To my friend Kay,

"With Love"

Beulah Stowers Fox

Beulah S. Fox

&

A Selection of
Short Stories
&
Poems

Published by
Holley's Printing
Pulaski, Tennessee
Copyright © 2001

In memory of my devoted parents
CLARA AND WILEY

Acknowledgements

To the people whose names are mentioned in the book.

To the hundreds of pupils I have taught through the years.

To two very special people, Jerry Fox Law, my daughter, and Shirley Richardson, my niece. Without them this book would not have been published. A special thanks also goes to Donald Law for editing and Peggy Mitchell for her help with publishing.

Warm thanks!

This book is dedicated to the loving memory of my beloved husband of more than fifty years, Elmer Lee Fox.

About the Author..

Beulah Stowers Fox, author of *With Love, & A Selection of Short Stories & Poems,* is a native of Bland County, Virginia. She resides at 709 Mercer Road, Rich Creek, Virginia. She has one daughter, Jerry Fox Law, ASID, who is employed by Marriott International as an Senior Interior Design Manager in the international division. Jerry is married to Robert W. Law, III. The couple resides in Rockville, Maryland and Bishopville, South Carolina. Mrs. Fox has two grandchildren, Jennifer Law Dahmen and Nelson Fox Law, both of Wake Forest, North Carolina. Mrs. Fox also has two great-grandchildren, Nicholas Law Dahmen and Sarah Christine Dahmen. Jennifer is married to Will Dahmen.

Mrs. Fox is a graduate of Rocky Gap High School, Rocky Gap, Virginia, Hiwassee College, at Madisonville, Tennessee. She received her B.S. Degree from Concord College, Athens, West Virginia and her Master's Degree from Virginia Polytechnic and State University at Blacksburg, Virginia. She is a member of the First United Methodist Church in Rich Creek, Virginia.

Her teaching experience has been in Bland and Giles Counties. She was principal for six years at Glen Lyn Elementary School, Glen Lyn, Virginia. Her hobbies are reading, writing and quilting.

Part I, *With Love*, published in 1976 was written as a tribute to her parents and grandparents as an appreciation of her heritage. It is a story of family life during the lean years of the thirties, which tells of struggles with hints of history and love of common things. Part II and III include a selection of more recent short stories and poems.

CONTENTS

CONTENTS

CONTENTS

INTRODUCTION

Someone has said, "Be careful of what you dream, for dreams have a way of coming true." I can not remember when I did not want to be a teacher. I can remember playing school with my brothers, sisters, and the neighbor's children in one corner of the wood shed. The others were the pupils and I was the teacher who stood in front while they sat on blocks of wood.

I graduated from high school as valedictorian in the Spring of 1936.

After much studying of college catalogs and with the help of my minister, the Rev. A. A. Angle, it was decided that I should attend Hiwassee College at Madisonville, Tennessee. Rev. Angle had helped me secure a job to help defray expenses, for money was scarce.

My father was a wounded veteran of World War I and drew a disability pension of twenty-seven dollars a month. In order for me to attend Hiwassee College he would have to send me nineteen dollars out of the twenty-seven dollars he received monthly. I worked in the laundry, dining hall, and as a janitor to earn the remaining ten dollars for tuition. Tuition was twenty-nine dollars a month. I had to find some way to earn money for books and other needed supplies. This I did by waving hair and hemming dresses. I was not allowed to charge for waving hair, but students paid me fifteen cents a head. The teachers and dieticians paid more. The nearest beauty shop was two miles away and this service was more convenient. I received ten cents ($0.10) for hemming dresses.

I had never been very far from home. Even though I loved Hiwassee dearly, at times I was a bit homesick and yearned for home and for my mother's home cooking.

I did not at any time fret because of scarcity of funds and clothes. I was doing what I had always wanted to do. My parents were making a sacrifice to allow me to do so.

In today's affluent society I suppose we would be called poor, but if we were poor we didn't know it. We had parents who loved us and we were rich in many ways, such as honesty, compassion for others, and the willingness to work hard.

In August 1974 I found some letters I had written home. Without the letters that my mother had saved I could not have remembered this much about this period of my life.

My daughter, Jerry, said, "Mother, save them. You may want to write a book sometime." A seed was planted.

At our home, Elmer's and mine, there always seems to be some sort of project going. One more wouldn't matter. When I first started I intended to record only the letters with comments about them for the enjoyment of our two grandchildren, Jennifer and Nelson. While I was writing I could almost hear Jennifer say, "But Grandmother, tell how it was when you were a little girl." Thus I have tried to "tell it like it was." I have included some of the letters in their exact words which I wrote my parents when I was away from home.

May it say to them the same thing I have said to many other boys and girls. "You can do whatever you want to do. The magic word is TRY!"

B. S. F.

Part One
With Love

Hollyhocks and Homemade Soap

There is nothing better for a man than that he should eat and drink and find enjoyment in his toil. EccI. 2:24.

My grandparents were born on the farm, so were my parents, and so was I. I was the oldest of eight children, all born at home. Since we lived on the same farm with my father's parents I can remember more about them than I can remember about my mother's parents.

The house my grandparents lived in was a two-story, unpainted, L-shaped house. It sat in the middle of a level yard which in summer was framed with hollyhocks of every color, lilacs, and orange day lilies. Along the road in front of the house grew wild phlox. These were the only flowers that I can remember my grandparents growing. My grandmother, Christina, loved hollyhocks so well that they were allowed to stand where they came up. Plank or board walks ran in different directions.

Grandma raised permelons. They were nurtured by making a hill or small mound of soil with manure in it, and grew over the garden fence, which was also the yard fence. Several permelons grew on each vine. These were put in the cellar for winter use.

Since I was the oldest grandchild I spent much time at my grandparents' house, across the foot log and up the road a short ways from our house. Grandma cooked almost all the food over the kitchen fireplace. Cabbage with red peppers was cooked half a day. She had a small mealroom, joining the kitchen, with barrels of flour and corn meal which came from grain raised on the hillsides. On the walls of the mealroom were shelves supported

1

by spools strung on a metal rod. Across the end of the wall were gourds of different sizes with round holes cut in front. In the gourds were ingredients for making bread. It always seemed to me that Grandma could go in the mealroom, turn around a time or two and come out with a pan full of biscuits ready for the oven. Biscuits were made from sour milk using soda for leavening. Baking powder was believed to be bad for the stomach and was never used. When the biscuits were baked they were peaked. I never remember eating there without the brown sugar syrup or the peaked biscuits. Along with this she might have chicken and dumplings, which seemed to be her speciality, hot raspberry pie with country butter on top, honey in a large square-covered dish, baked melons, and country butter. A newspaper placed around a stick like a flag and slit into tiny strips was used to "shoo" the flies away. Sheets of sticky fly paper was also used.

In the corner of the kitchen behind the door that led into the big dining room was a table opposite the Home Comfort stove. On the table were all kinds of homemade brass bells, cow bells of different sizes, sheep bells, and turkey bells. I enjoyed ringing one of these bells to call the others at mealtime.

Grandma washed under some willow trees next to the creek which ran in front of her house. Uncle Grat was the youngest boy and helped her with the washing. Grandma kept wondering what was happening to his socks. Every wash day a few more seemed to disappear. Uncle Grat did not enjoy wearing darned or patched socks. So every week he burned a few in the fire under the iron pot in which the water was heated. Grandma finally caught him in the act.

Neither could Grandma read or write. She had learned to count by counting eggs. She kept the egg money in a tin half-gallon syrup can.

One day Grandma surprised everybody. For years she had washed on the board. On this day an agent came through the country selling Maytag washing machines, the gray ones with the gasoline motors. Grandma "took a liking to it." She usually asked Will about any major purchase. Not this time! She went to her corner cupboard and brought enough money out to pay for the washing machine with a little left over. "Now God I say," that was her word, "I'm going to have me one of those things. I've washed on the board long enough." "Will", that was my Grandpa, "needn't say anything about it. I paid for it."

The wainscoting in the big room was painted a barn red. The remainder of the walls and the ceiling were white plaster. It was full of furniture with one full-sized bed, one half bed, dresser, washstand, and a small table with a cubby-hole box on top with doors on it that could be locked, which was Grandpa's desk. The desk sat in a corner next to the window. On a shelf under the table were stacked Sears Catalogs from previous years, and around the room were several straight-back chairs. Lace curtains covered the windows and pieces of oil cloth were used as scarves on the furniture. Five clocks sat on the mantlepiece. They were never allowed to stop running and never seemed to be quite together, one ticking, then another ticking, striking on the hour and the half hour. Round rag rugs covered the floor.

The record player sat in front of the washstand. Young people gathered here on Saturday night and listened to the records. WILDWOOD FLOWER was very popular. One record that I remember was DON'T EVER BOB YOUR HAIR, GIRLS. At that time and until I was a senior in high school, I had long hair. So I was teased a great deal about this particular song. We sat around the fireplace while the fire blazed and crackled, listened to the songs, and sometimes popped corn.

My mother made most of Grandma's clothes. Grandma would ride in the buggy to the country store, buy a bolt of fabric and have all of the fabric made into dresses and aprons. The dresses were all made alike; so were the aprons. The dresses were ankle length. The aprons were gathered at the top to a band that tied behind and were also ankle length. Grandma loved the color red. The dresses would be red, black and white, or blue and white checked gingham.

Grandma was outspoken. Not everybody approved of this characteristic of hers. Once she received an ugly valentine showing a woman with a big mouth. Instead of complaining about the valentine she enjoyed it and put it on the wall above the table, where everybody could view it.

At Grandma's my room was a little room joining the big room.

When I spent the night with Grandma I crawled up, placing feet in between straw and feather ticks, until I reached the top of the lot and sank down in the middle of the feather ticks. The straw ticks were on the bottom. Then on cold winter nights because there was no heat in the room, she wrapped a heated iron in cloth and put it at my feet and tucked them in. Even now I enjoy my feet tucked in.

Grandma thought if her house was painted all of the preachers would stop for dinner. She'd always laugh when she said this. However, she probably fed as many preachers as anyone else and they seemed to feel welcome.

The cellar was built into the side of a hill. I can remember being sent to the cellar, which was about a block from the house, for cans of fruits and vegetables. Grandma always called it the apple house. The door had sawdust inside and was very thick and heavy. It was all that I could do to get it pushed open so I could get the things she wanted. The attic part of the cellar was not enclosed from the back. You could climb the hill, crawl inside, and play.

One time when her son was getting married she said, "Go tell your Mother to come over here. Randall is going to 'jump the broomstick'. That puzzled me. I ran home and asked Mother what 'jumping the broomstick' meant.

There was always a lot of patching to do. Grandma never wasted anything. Yet that big heart of hers was just as generous as could be if she could share something with someone who needed it. When she patched anything dark she used white thread. When she patched anything light she used dark thread. I think she could see her work better that way. She never wore glasses.

One time she had a hen to steal her nest out and bring in one little chicken. Winter was coming. Instead of bringing the chickens inside Grandma took care of it another way. She looked at me and said, "Go fetch my scissors and the overall patches." I obeyed. She looked at the chicken and then she cut and sewed a garment to fit it. There may have been other chickens born late in the fall, but I bet this was the only chicken in Clearfork Valley that wore a neat little pair of overalls. I can't remember whether the chicken survived the cold weather or not. But, knowing Grandma, I would say that it did.

4

She also took care of little baby lambs. I loved to watch the little lambs play on the hillside. Many times I begged Daddy to let us have some sheep. He always thought they were too much trouble. We never had any of our own.

Besides all of the other things my Grandma did, she made her own soap. First a hole was bored in the bottom of a wooden barrel, then the barrel was set on a bench. Some straw was put in the barrel with fresh wood ashes on top of the straw. When the barrel was nearly full of ashes, water was poured over the ashes. A brown liquid would drip out the hole. This was the lye she used in making the family's soap.

When a mother who had a baby or small child came visiting Grandma and the mother would usually slip over to our house to use our soap for bathing.

You've heard of "kissin' cousins." One day one of my Grandma's cousins from Nebraska came to see her. The man called her Aunt Christina and put his arm around her. Immediately she slapped his face and said, "Now God I say, no strange man's going to do me that way."

I would sit for hours looping strips of cloth together while Grandma hooked rugs. Rugs overlapped each other in the big room, never called the parlor. Regardless of the number of rugs she had she continued hooking rugs with a wooden hook Grandpa had made for her. I enjoyed hearing the ticking of the clocks while we worked.

The church record that was transcribed by the Rev. S.K. Byrd, June 3, 1887 showed that Grandma joined Mt. Nebo Methodist Church sometime prior to this date, her name being the twenty-eighth name on this early church record. She never missed a service unless she was too sick to attend. She'd put on her best dress, a new apron, her best bonnet tied under her chin, and her high-topped shoes. A safety pin seemed to be always present at the neck of her dress. Then she rode horseback, on a side saddle, to church. To get to church she had to ride around a hill, which rose abruptly on the other side of the creek, about two miles from where she lived. This path wound around by chestnut trees, full of chestnuts in the fall of the year, and led to a small white church on top of the hill. She always sat in the front row.

"What was the use of a body going to church if a body had to sit so far back she can't hear," she'd say. When she got happy, and this was almost every time, she would shout. As she shouted her bonnet came off and went back over the crowd toward the rear of the church.

When others questioned why certain things happened Grandma always said, "The good Lord planned it that way." Grandma was superstitious, but one thing she didn't believe in was Groundhog's Day. Many people believed if the groundhog saw his shadow there would be six more weeks of bad weather. Grandma always said, "The good Lord never put the weather in the hands of a groundhog."

As Grandma got older she suffered gall bladder attacks. She would ring a bell for help. Sometimes we crawled the foot log across the creek, when the water was high, to help or get help for her.

On March 13, 1936 she went home with God. No one knew exactly how old she was. Some people thought she was 79 years of age, but others thought she was much older. I shall always remember her as one who did what she could to make things better and one who accepted the things she could do nothing about.

Grandma and Grandpa Stowers in front of the hollyhocks they loved so well.

Grandpa's Stories

My father and Grandfather must have been disappointed that I was born a girl. I'm sure they could have used a boy to help with the farm chores. So at an early age I learned to work both outside and inside. During the summer of 1923 I carried water to my grandfather in the hay fields. He asked me what size socks I wore. I told him I wore size four. Since I was four years old, I thought I wore size four. Black seemed to be the only color made. He bought size four for me and they were much too small. How disappointed I was until I learned that merchandise could be exchanged. This was my first paying job.

Many times Grandpa would slip us a big stick of peppermint candy. I'd run to meet him and check about the candy.

Later I learned how to throw hay to the cows, gather eggs, and milk with both hands playing a rhythm with the milk and bucket.

My Grandfather was perhaps not as colorful as Grandmother. What I remember most about him were the stories he told me. The best remembered story that he told me was one that may have come from McGuffey's Reader and went like this: Once there was a man who had six sons. The man called his sons to him and said, "Sons, I want each of you to bring me a stick." The sons did as they were asked. The father took each stick and broke one stick at a time. Then he said, "Now bring me six more sticks." The sons did as requested. This time the father bound all six sticks together. He tried to break the bundle and could not. Then Grandfather would say, "This is how families should stick together."

I have also heard this story. This story was related to my Grandfather by Dr. Hicks on Clearfork. Dr. Hicks was going to see a patient when he saw Uncle Grat sitting on a gate. Dr. Hicks said Uncle Grat was about four or five years old when he hailed him and said, "Doc, would you do something for me this morning? I'm sick."

Doc said, "Grat, what's wrong with you?"

"I didn't eat my thirteenth biscuit for breakfast this morning."

Doc said, "By gosh Grat, you ought to be dead."

When molasses-making time came Grandpa cut cane stalks that could be used for licking the molasses pan.

Daddy, Mother, a cousin Thelma, Donald, Phyllis, and Barbara making molasses.

Grandpa was over in the meadow putting up hay when I caught my first Red-Eye. I don't know which one was more excited, he or I. He came running across the foot-log and up to where I was saying, "The poor fish, you pulled him out so

8

hard you blinded him". Then he showed me a better way to land a fish.

One time Grandpa and I went up on the mountain to a peach orchard, which was part of the farm. We had ridden a horse up the mountain. The peaches were poured into sacks and laid across the horse. As we came down the mountain the horse stumbled and fell on the gravels. My Father said later, "No wonder he fell, Grandpa was big, plus you, and the peaches."

Grandpa was very lonely after Grandma died. He lived only two years after she died. On the twenty-first day of June, while working in the wheat field, he became sick and died soon afterwards.

I had always heard that Grandfather was eighteen years and my Grandmother was thirty-six years old when they were married. I often wondered why she wouldn't always be twice as old as my Grandfather.

"Baby Ray Has A Dog"

It was the fall of 1924. One of my earliest recollections was when I was five years old. I walked a mile to school with my Aunt Ada, Mother's sister. Aunt Ada boarded at our home. I was chubby and short. It was hard to keep up with her as she held my hand. Enrollment age was six. With special permission I was allowed to attend school but was not allowed to complete the first grade that year. Aunt Ada was a "natural-born", teacher. She taught grades 1-7. I'm sure that my admiration for my aunt contributed greatly to my desire of becoming a teacher. She loved all children and they loved her. She enjoyed telling that the first word I ever spelled for her was cunning. It came from the Baby Ray Book.

Later I remember the Blue Back Spelling Book and the Elson Gray Readers. One of my favorite stories was "The King of the Golden River."

School was fun. Some of the games played were, making playhouses under a walnut tree behind the school house, playing Aunty-Over, Leap Frog, What Time Is It, Old Witch? and Jack Rocks. When we played house we petitioned rooms by arranging rocks in the form of a house plan, used dried leaves for fried ham meat and weeds for vegetables. Our jack rocks were pebbles polished by nature. We treasured a set of pebbles of the right size for jack rocks. We played on the tin, left over from covering the school building. The tin was stored under the school house which was not under-penned. We pulled out the tin, used it to play on, and put it back before the bell rang.

During those early years of school we were not as safety-conscious as we are now. I can remember a seventh grade boy who rode a white horse to school, pinching the horse on the rump making it rear up and kick. Pupils scattered quickly. In the winter time old tubs were used for sleighs in which we rode down a high hill behind the school. Jumping the branch was common at recess time, usually known as Follow the Leader.

Then we got in line and marched in to our double desks. I was quiet in school. One time it was all I could do to keep from laughing. A boy who sat behind me was telling this tale: A farmer had lost his hogs. He searched and searched for them. Finally he came to a hollow tree. One of the hog's tails stuck out of the base of the tree. The farmer pulled the tail and out came forty-four of the missing hogs. The boy could tell it without grinning. The ones who laughed were punished.

Home Sweet Home

Our house was a four-room house, two rooms downstairs and two rooms upstairs, no porches. The kitchen door led to the outside with a large rock on which to step just outside the door and a plank walk leading to the yard gate. There were about five steps leading from the front door. It was fun to sit on the front steps and peak through the holes trying to see what treasures were under the steps. My father said the holes were there where the knots fell out. It was funny to me that trees had knots. You had to wait until just before the sun went down, then the light showed underneath the steps. There were glass beads, safety pins, and buttons. Sometimes I liked to sit on the steps and look at the world around me.

The inside of the house was covered with heavy brown paper, the nails going through shiny metal discs which held the paper to the wall. On the paper upstairs was written the names of the family that had lived in the house before my father and mother moved there following the end of World War I.

Later my mother papered the house with clean newspapers using flour paste. It looked nice and clean after the papering. The picture on the wall I remember most was a picture of the Guardian Angel watching a little girl crossing a bridge over a swollen stream of water.

On the wall was a rectangle-shaped phone. Our ring was four longs. This was four long rings. Since we were on a party line every family had to have a special ring. Each family serviced his own poles. My father serviced twelve poles. My father believed in progress. Our family was among the first families in the valley to have a phone, electric lights, and water. Our water came from a spring about a mile from the house. Daddy laid the pipe around the hill. It still comes from the same place today.

In the fall we had wood-cuttings. Neighbors gathered, hooked a tractor to a wood saw, and cut enough wood for the winter ahead. At night we dug the wood out of the winter's quilt of white, carried it inside, and placed it in the wood box. It was comforting to have plenty of wood on a cold wintry day.

I learned early about the birds and bees. My parents always wrote on the calendar when the cows could expect calves. My sisters, brothers, and I soon learned to interpret the writing on the calendar.

Beulah, Ruth and W. H. in front of house.

Bringing in the turkeys, ducks and the cows were our

chores. One foggy morning I remember making this verse, "When the fog veils East River Mountain, and fills the valley far and wide. It's then that I see God in nature and feel his presence by my side."

All was not work. We had fun picking branches of locust blossoms for a table bouquet. It was believed that locust trees attracted lightning. We remembered to stay away from the tree if it were lightning. Wild red and yellow columbine abounded on the cliffs, near the spring. Yellow roses grew up the hollow, where at one time an old house was located. We hid eggs at Easter. We gathered hickory nuts, beech nuts, chestnuts and walnuts. May apples were gathered and eaten. Mullen and wild cherry bark were used for cough syrup. Homemade horehound candy was also used for coughs.

Daddy's Quarter Round

My father was a farmer
Who liked to till the sod
He grafted trees and tended bees
And fought in the war across the seas.

In the year of 1940 he remodeled our house and built four more rooms to the front, thus doubling its original size. At that time nine windows 14 x 28 cost $2.94 each, totaling $26.46. Six 8-1/2 x 8-1/2 flu linings cost thirty-three cents each. Daddy always liked things convenient, or handy as he would say. So we had two front doors.

One front door went into the living room and one door went into the dining room. Sheet rock was used for walls and ceiling. Daddy did everything except hang the doors. He was not a carpenter by trade. When he made a mistake he covered it with a piece of quarter round. He always said, "Quarter-round can hide a multitude of sins." We had a saying around our house, "If you make a mistake use a piece of quarter round."

I was given a room of my own, the upstairs front west room. I chose this room because I enjoyed the sunset from the window.

Daddy had a story he liked to tell called EVERYBODY'S HOUSE. It went like this: A man was building a house. Neighbors came by and said, "I'd put the window on this side or the chimney on the other end or the door on the other side." The man made all the changes.

A few days later neighbors came by and saw the man building another house. The neighbors asked, "Why are you building another house?"

The man replied, "That was everbody's house. This is my house." Daddy told us this when we asked him to make only one front door.

One of the things I enjoyed doing was helping my father in his blacksmith shop. Sometimes I pumped the bellows to make the fire hotter. I always liked to use tongs and carry the hot horseshoes, that had just been turned, to the creek behind the shop. There I would put them in the water and listen to them sizzle.

Our horses' names were always Maude and Nell. Nell was more gentle than Maude. Daddy also rented corn fields. My sisters, brothers, and I hoed corn in fields touching each other for a mile and a half up the road. Sometimes the fields were very rocky. Corn had to be hilled, that is fresh soil piled around each hill of corn. I remember one time we had a hard time moving the rocks to find enough soil for the hilling. Brambles were common.

Part of the time we ate in the field. Ruth, (my sister), and I would go to the house and bring back the dinner bucket full of food. The dinner bucket had a cup on top and compartments inside. Mother would have fried pies and other goodies packed with a jug of cold sweet milk to drink.

Sometimes while in the fields we would hear the ringing of a cowbell. This meant to come home. Bees were swarming. Daddy taught me how to put on his bee outfit and save the bees. To do this I climbed the ladder, cut off the branch with about a gallon of bees hanging on it, and took it down to the front of the new hive or home. If you could find the queen and put her in the first the others would follow. I've watched the bees do many interesting things, such as two bees carrying out the dead ones, dropping him and bringing out others the same way.

Our family loved company. Daddy used to take the spring wagon up to Aunt Ellen's, (Grandma's sister) and bring her to visit us for the day or for several days. She could never say my name correctly and always called me Julie.

Daddy enjoyed visiting his kin; aunts, uncles, and cousins. Periodically he made his rounds. I have the feeling that he enjoyed this more than Mother did. Daddy was very out-going.

I helped Daddy graft trees. If a twig from an apple tree is carefully inserted in a slit made in the bark of another apple tree the twig will grow. Daddy ran some grafting wax around the tree to seal it. He liked to experiment with his trees in the orchard. On one tree he had seven different kinds of apples growing. A twig taken from a tree when grafted into another tree will produce the same kind of fruit borne by the tree from which it was taken. Apples will not grow from oak trees.

Daddy called it "peddlin'." Vegetables and fruits were loaded the night before. About 3 o'clock in the morning my Daddy and I would get up and eat breakfast. Then we would leave in the spring wagon to go to Bluefield. All Daddy had to do to sell his vegetables was to pull up a hollow and stop. People would come from all directions to buy. Daddy always believed in good measure. He called it "heaping it up and running it over." He said somewhere in the Bible it said to do it this way.

A car salesman came to our house one day and sold Daddy a model A Ford. The salesman drove the car up the road and

Daddy drove it back. Daddy was more at home with horses, buggies, and wagons than he was with a car. He was always an awkward driver. However, I suppose the only wreck he had was when he drove off the road in the fog and turned the car over. No one was hurt.

Evelyn and Model A Ford.

17

Sacrifice and Joy

Mother and Bud, our new house which my father built.

My mother did not have an easy time with eight children. Especially did she have a hard time giving birth to twins at home. In fact she was so ill that the doctor said she had one

18

chance in a thousand getting better. The twins were girls, Phyllis Jean and Barbara Dean. They weighed exactly two and one-half pounds each. Ruth took Barbara to care for and I took Phyllis. We put them on a pillow in a can box, with a hot water bottle under the pillow. Then we took turns sitting up half a night each to watch them. They survived. Ruth stayed out of school the remainder of that year so that I could graduate from high school.

Mother put up many cans of food to fill empty stomachs. She and I loved crabapple jelly. We walked several miles to pick the crabapples so she could make jelly.

Under a tree in the front yard Mother washed all day once a week to get our clothes clean. Then she ironed with irons heated on top of the stove.

Mother taught me many things that I still enjoy. She taught me how to crochet and embroider. Feed sacks were cut into squares and designs were stamped on the squares. It was very special to have a piece of fabric ready to embroider. She had a sewing machine. Daddy had bought the sewing machine for her from money earned from selling turkeys.

In the spring of the year we cut spicewood branches and swept the yard. Never did it look so pretty. We also used the spicewood branches to brush our teeth.

In late summer we helped Mother cook for thrashers. Dozens of apple and custard pies were made, besides gallons of vegetables, plenty of ham, and chicken and dumplings. The thrashers went from house to house thrashing grain. Daddy helped everyone who helped him.

Blading sugar cane was no easy job. The whole family worked at this. No matter what you wore the blades seemed to cut through to the skin. At first we made molasses in a pan. Later we used an evaporator which made better molasses. One time the molasses got too thick and we poured it into the creek. All of the children who were watching immediately went wading through the sticky goo.

In winter Mother took clean snow and made snow cream for us. We made taffy and popped corn. At Christmas time we hung our stockings and got an orange in the toe. We were told we'd get a switch in our stockings if we were mean.

Mother played the organ and we sang around it. The song I remember most was "Red River Valley." Sometimes she played "Life is Like a Mountain Railroad" and "Shall We Gather at the River?" These last two songs were Daddy's favorite hymns. She also played a song that her father loved, "I Met a Wayward Stranger". Mother had attended singing schools when she was a young girl and she had a good soprano voice.

Mother once wrote this poem which she called "Part of Life"-

Behind the hills of old Virginia
The sun sinks slowly out of sight
Leaving clouds of red and silver
Reflecting the last rays of night.
Purple shadows of the twilight
Deeper in the valley grows;
Then the morn in all her splendor
O'er East River Mountain shows.
Bathing all the land in beauty
Scattering rays of golden light,
Then the glory of the sunset
Fades as magic in to night.

Clara Stowers

Twins and Donald

20

Fruitcake and Peppermint

My first year of high school was in a one-room school, the teacher teaching three of us after she had taught grades one to seven all day. We went to school three hours after the regular school day. Miss Trula carried books to us. I can still remember part of Sir Walter Scott's, "Lady of the Lake" because she made the story come alive. She was an excellent teacher.

The new high school had been built at Rocky Gap by this time, but no bus came by our house. So the next year I lived with mother's parents, Sallie and J. W. Walters, at Rocky Gap and attended Rocky Gap High School.

Grandma and Grandpa Walters.

I can remember Grandmother sewing for me. She was good at matching colors and trimmings. I was very proud of the dresses she made me. On cold winter nights she made vegetable soup. I would go to the cellar for her and bring back vegetables and canned tomatoes to go into the soup. Nobody made better soup than my grandmother. I can remember walking up to the top of the high hill to the milk gap with her, and helping carry the milk to the house. Grandmother brought laughter when she read Uncle Remus stories. Sometimes she made us a Fox and Geese board, so we could play this game.

One of the sweetest memories I have was the family-get-together at Christmas time at Grandpa and Grandmother's house. The family would often gather on Christmas Eve. Beds would be full. Grandchildren slept on pallets on the floor. Every Christmas Grandmother made her old time fruitcake. It was simply a thin stack cake made with molasses in it with apple butter filling. It could have many layers. We looked forward to Grandmother's fruitcake.

Grandpa always had boxes of peppermint candy. Anyone who came near him got a stick of peppermint candy.

In the front room was a battery radio. After supper we ate apples from a pan while listening to Amos and Andy, Lum and Abner, Jam-Up and Honey, and Sarah and Sally. The evening was not complete until Grandpa had listened to Lowell Thomas with the news.

The third and fourth years of high school I stayed home. By that time there was a bus that came part of the way up Clearfork Valley. It was at this time that I walked two miles through the mud, carrying my lantern, to get on the bus. The year after I graduated from high school the bus came by our door.

Keeping Up With The Plow

I remember still the days of spring plowing, the smell of the earth, springtimes refreshing shower, and the odor of fresh cut hay.

It was the summer of 1936. My brothers, sisters and I were in the cornfield planting beans and pumpkin seeds. When we planted the pumpkin seeds Daddy would say, "Drop two in the hill. If you drop three, don't stoop to pick it up. If you drop four, bend your back and pick it up." It seemed that we dropped the pumpkin seed rather quickly. I couldn't help but wonder if William Hicks had dropped all of his seeds. We were glad when we finished planting the pumpkin seeds. Now we could drop the beans. It was fun to drop beans for they would slip out of your hands easier than the pumpkin seeds.

Daddy always told us to do a good job but try to keep up with the plow. To him, keeping up with the plow meant not to get too far behind with whatever you were doing. In this instance it meant to stay as close as you could behind the plow.

About the middle of the morning he would hunt us what he called a dark spot and we would rest in the shade of a tree. I remember resting under a poplar tree, full of bloom and looking like a tree of yellow tulips. When we could step on our shadow it was time to go home for lunch.

How good it felt to lie on the cold linoleum floor in the bedroom while Mother was placing the food on the table. Mother had lunch almost ready, raspberry pie, sweet cold milk from the spring house, chicken and dumplings, apples, honey, other vegetables, and fruits raised on the farm. Even the wheat and corn used in bread were grown on the farm.

The corn had to be hoed four times. Soil had to be raked

around each hill. If the rows started out short and got longer I took the longest row. Ruth, just younger than I, took the next longest and W. H. took the shortest one, for he was the youngest of the three of us. Daddy believed in being fair about these things.

Later that summer I remember hearing Daddy say "To be sure your sins will find you out." W. H. hadn't dropped the pumpkins, two in a hill. He had hid them in a rock pile. The seeds grew and the vines covered the rock pile.

As a special treat when the hoeing was done Daddy would take us in a cave or go fishing with us. Usually we'd explore a cave. Now I think of the danger and wonder why we did it. Then it was fun!

Ruth was good about wearing the bonnet Mother made her, but I never wore mine. I'd start out wearing mine and then take it off. Mother finally realized it was useless to insist on me wearing it and bought me a straw hat.

I had graduated as valedictorian from Rocky Gap High School that spring. Long before that I had decided what I wanted to do. More than anything else I wanted to teach boys and girls. I knew that money was scarce, but if I were given an opportunity I would make the most of it. So that summer I worked and waited.

It was an early August morning. I hadn't slept much the night before. The family was seated around the breakfast table. I could tell that Mother was a bit sad about my leaving for school. I had not been away from home except to spend some time with grandparents and aunts. Daddy had cut a ham for breakfast. I didn't feel much like eating, for when the day came to leave I, too, had mixed emotions. I wanted to go to school but I loved the farm. I had never been away from home that long before.

Daddy took me in his model A Ford to Bluefield to go by bus to Madisonville, Tenn. I was to change buses at Knoxville. In the fog, on his way back home, he missed the road and turned the car over into the creek. No one was hurt.

I was on my way to college. I planned to pursue without fail the road to my ideals. A few days later my parents received a letter.

A New Experience

Dear Mother,

The bus ride was great. I didn't get sick. I arrived at Bristol at *9:15* and at Knoxville, Tenn. at 12:20. There was no bus going to Madisonville until 4:30. When we stopped at Knoxville I gave the check to the ticket agent to pay for my ticket. He would not take it or give me a ticket. I didn't know what to do. I sat awhile and then talked to him again, and again, and again. Finally he got so tired of seeing and hearing me that he said, "Show me some identification." I went down to the baggage room. It was very dark in there. After falling over all kinds of baggage I found my foot locker and unlocked it. There I found a receipt Mr. Colston, the college president, had sent me.

Then I told the agent, "If the president of a college could accept a check for five dollars, could you not accept one for one dollar and eighty cents." Finally he agreed.

A few minutes later our bus was being loaded for Madisonville.

Madisonville is a small town. A taxi met us. The driver took two of us and our baggage for seventy-five cents. This was lower than half price. I had told him I was working my way through school. I arrived at the college at 7:20.

Mrs. Helvey, the housemother, met me and showed me to my room, no. 17. She is Mrs. Mattie Repass's niece, at Hollybrook. The others had already eaten but she fixed me a snack.

My room is nice. It has one dresser, double bed, mantle piece, library table, and a closet for my things.

It's a lovely, lovely place!

The teachers and girls are so friendly.

Guess what my work is! I have a job ironing. I have to iron only on Tuesdays, Wednesdays, and Thursdays. I do not have to work on week-ends. The laundry is under the dining hall. Clothes are washed on Monday. I am ironing dresses and shirts, about sixty a week. Any time we have a free period we can iron and then go back to class.

The doctor is going to examine us about Saturday, I think. If I had known I had to have an examination, I could have had it before I came down here.

Well, I didn't get a part in the play. I was glad because our choir director told us last night that the choir had an invitation to sing at the Hoiston Conference, Cleveland, Tennessee. This is the same place the play is to be given. I'd rather sing than be in the play. This is to be Oct. 9. The choir is supposed to sing two songs. I plan to go. I shall wear my swagger suit. Of course we have robes to wear in the choir. All of the robes are alike. This, I think, will be a great experience for me. Don't you? Wonder if I could sing before so many people. Tell Rev. Angle I am looking forward to seeing.

THURSDAY

It is necessary that I pay nineteen dollars tuition tomorrow. Mr. Colston said not to pay it later than the second. The nineteen dollars will have to be in the bank. I will give the check late Friday evening and trust that it will be ok.

The doctor from Madisonville came out Tuesday and examined us. Several had heart trouble. I don't think they were sent home. He told me my fingers were more crooked than any he had ever seen. I wanted to ask him if I paid him to tell me that. He really examined us, even to our toes. He said, "The only think wrong with you is that you are from Virginia." I told him I was very proud of that fact.

I am studying grammar. This is hard for me. I haven't studied grammar since I was in the eighth grade. Don't know what I am making on psychology. You will get my grades at the end of three months.

I study every day except Sunday from 9-10, from 1:30-4:30, and from 7:00-10:30. The lights are turned off at 10:30.

On Tuesdays I iron from 9-10 and sometimes in the afternoon.

I have to buy another English book for seventy-five cents *($0.75)*. I have enough change to buy it, I think, without writing a check.

The second quarter starts about the middle of November. I will take Bible then. I may write later for you to mail my Bible to me. It must be a revised edition. Look and see if mine is a revised edition.

I made a talk on Thursday on "Greater Love Hath No Man Than This." I have to give another talk on Oct. 13. This is one thing I'm learning to do, talk before an audience. I think this is of great value to anyone.

Send me Aunt Ruth's address and I'll write her a card.

You wrote about the small senior class at Rocky Gap. I thought our class of six people would hold the record for being the smallest class. Now it won't be the smallest.

I'm sure every class at Rocky Gap thinks its rings are the prettiest. That's natural. Mine is as pretty as any I've seen down here.

I do hope you get a new auditorium. It is much needed.

I've been begging Mother Helvey to come in with us at Christmas time. I don't know whether she will or not.

I'd love to see the twins. And Phyllis Jean has curly hair! Can both of them talk?

Take good care of yourself.

With love,
Beulah

P.S. Send me a stamp, please.

27

Perhaps I was naive in thinking I could get a check cashed where I was not known. My father always taught us, "A man's word is as good as his bond." He believed this and I'm sure he didn't foresee any problem of getting his check cashed. He trusted everyone. This was the way I was taught.

A swagger suit was a skirt with a three-quarter length coat. At the present time this outfit would be in style.

Works In Laundry

I have just finished ironing. I only had thirty shirts. It is easy to iron about twenty an hour. I am afraid to finish too soon, Mr. Coiston might find me another job. So I have taken my time.

So many of the girls here dread practice teaching. I am looking forward to it, but I won't get to take it until next year.

Just finished my English test. It wasn't as hard as I expected it to be.

Received your letter this morning, Ruth. I'm glad you're going in the second year. Bet you are sorry you don't have any classes under Mr. Reynolds. I sure am. Most teachers down here use southern dialect. They don't pronounce their r's. Mr. Reynolds is as good a teacher as can be found. Oh well, maybe I'll get used to that southern drawl.

Evelyn, I'm so glad you like French. What does this mean, Comment-t-allez-vous au jourd'hui? Learn to speak it well, and we will talk some at Christmas time.

I'm so glad the girls in our senior class are going to college. Our senior class is showing up well, I think. All are in school except one. It's good news hearing that the bus comes by our door. That's better than walking four miles a day, in the mud, carrying my lantern.

No, I am not gaining but I have lost two pounds.

Thinking of food, wouldn't I like to have a piece of that watermelon you were writing about.

You asked if I needed anything. Yes, you might send me a

stamp and my brown tam. It is getting cooler here now.

Take good care of yourself.

Love,

Hiwassee College is a junior college. Your second year was called your senior year. How I envied the seniors because they could do their student teaching. It was called practice teaching then.

I had not been far from home and thought the accents were strange.

Expenses, Expenses

Saturday
Sept. 26, 1936

Dear Daddy and all,

I am writing again in regard to the money for this month's tuition, nineteen dollars. Mr. Colston announced in Chapel (assembly) this morning that tuition was supposed to be paid at least by Monday. That's the 29th of this month. I have already paid for the first month. This is going on the second month. I don't know how you meant for me to pay. I am going to see Mr. Coiston in a few minutes and ask if it will be all right to pay mine on the second of October. Will it be all right to give a check for it them? Write and let me know. I've worked out ten dollars. This makes the twenty-nine dollars.

Just saw Mr. Colston. He told me I could pay the second of every month, although the others are supposed to pay Monday.

What have the twins been doing? Can they talk any? I'd like to see them.

I am in psychology class now. I like this class. Miss Bryson gives a lecture each day. I must stop writing during her class.

Try to stay well.

Love,
P. S. Enclosed is a list of my expenses for the month of September.

EXPENSES
September 1936

Bus fare, Bluefield to Knoxville	$4.35
Knoxville to Madisonville	.70
Madisonville to Hiwassee College	.38
Total	$5.43
Tuition, Board, etc.	14.00
Key deposit	.50
2 notebook fillers (I brought 2 from home)	.10
1 notebook	.05
2 composition books	.10
2 pencils brought from home	
1 psychology book (second-hand)	.88
1 French book (second-hand)	.65
1 English book (I had to buy this new)	1.30
1 English Practice Leaf, new	.65
Total	$23.66

I have given checks for $14.00, $3.65, $1.80, $1.75, $2.00 and $1.50. This amounts to $24.70. Subtracting the $23.66 from $24.70, this gives me $1.04 change. Then subtracting the $24.70 from the $30.00 you put in the bank, I now have $5.30 in the Bland Bank.

My father received his veteran's check on the first day of each month. My tuition was due on the first day of each month. After talking it over with the president he made an exception to the rule and thereafter I paid my tuition on the second day of each month.

I was thrifty. I had to be. Notice the bus fare from Bluefield to Knoxville and taxi fare from Madisonville to the college. Composition books were five cents each. Throughout the year I kept a strict account of money spent.

Sends Flowers By Mail

Oct. 31, 1936

Dearest Mother,

I received your flowers and letter Wednesday morning. The dahlias were not even wilted. We do not have any flowers here except cosmoses. We are not allowed to pick them. Dahlias are still pretty. I change the water on them every day. After cleaning my room this morning I placed one bunch of flowers on the dresser and one on the table. Thanks so much for sending them to me. It was very thoughtful of you.

It has been very cool here the last few days.

Yes, I do need a pair of black slippers. I meant to write you the last time I wrote and tell you I needed a pair. I could get them here, but I don't have any spare time. I'd like to have a pair of black lace oxfords, size 6-. Everybody wears them here. I haven't worn my new black dress but a few times since I didn't have any black slippers. I wore it when I gave my talk at prayer meeting.

When you send my slippers you could send me a notebook filler, too. I'm out of paper and I don't have any change.

Mother Helvey said she didn't think it would be possible for her to leave at Christmas time. She may change her mind. No, she doesn't have any children in school.

Bert wrote me that the twins were sick. Hope they are better.

Ruth, I don't have time to get up that order. I'm so busy.

I taught school an hour last Saturday, second grade. It was fun.

We are having a Halloween Carnival Saturday night. Everybody is supposed to dress "tacky," teachers included.

Since there was a teacher's meeting at Knoxville today, I didn't have but two classes.

We have a football game this evening, Hiwassee against Sneed College, Boaz, Georgia.

Daddy, are you one of the judges at the election this year? I have been reading about the election in the Knoxville Journal. The Literary Digest took a straw vote. The result was in favor of Landon. It has never failed to predict the president. I wonder if it will this time! Let me tell you about this! We had an election in school yesterday. The result was Roosevelt 126 votes, Landon 41. You can somewhat account for this since the South usually goes democratic. Our French teacher, from Louisiana, asked how many democrats there were in his class. He promised to give A's to the democrats and F's to the republicans. I bet!

Just think the next presidential election Beulah can vote. I am looking forward to that.

I am pleased to tell you that I made the honor roll this month.

It is just six more weeks until we get out for Christmas.

Daddy, it would be a nice trip for you to come for me at Christmas time. Wish you could come for me.

Ruth, look in Compton's Encyclopedia at Rocky Gap and any other place you know about for information about World Peace, a page will be enough. Get something about the cost of World War I in dollars and number of lives lost. Send it soon. I can get the other information here. Send it soon. Thanks.

Our football team won 17-0.

My grades for the second month were French B-Plus, Psychology B-Plus, and English B. I made the Honor Roll.

Mother, thanks again for the beautiful flowers.

Love to all,

Monday Morn.

Sorry I didn't get to mail it Saturday but missed the mail.

Miss Bryson took her Geography class on a trip to Lookout Mountain at Chattanooga, Tennessee. I have the day off.

Mother would you send me a pair of dark blue anklets? I'd like a pair to wear with my blue skirt.

I have just finished my washing. I didn't have but a few things.

Have a lot of studying to do, also some hair to wave.

With Love,

I shall always remember the flowers my mother sent me as one of the dearest things she did for me. She loved her dahlias and traded bulbs with the neighbors to get different colors. At other times she mailed me boxes of chinquapins, chestnuts, cake and candy.

Slippers, as they were called, were hard to get. At home you didn't wear out shoes. You wore a hole through the sole. Then Daddy got out the shoe last and put on a new sole. He did a good job of "halfsoling". Recycling was popular then, too. It just wasn't called that.

My father for years had been one of the judges at the election. He had made the ballot box with a lock on the outside. This made an impression on me and I looked forward to the time I could vote. In fact, I walked two miles to see if my name was on the list of registered voters. It was.

I was getting enough hair to wave to pay for small expenses. I was also doing alterations in my spare time. This helped too.

I cannot imagine ever wearing a $6\frac{1}{2}$ shoe. How my foot has grown!

Thanksgiving 1936

Dear Mother,

I don't have anything to do this evening but keep the radiator warm. It surely doesn't keep us warm. It has been snowing some here today. I haven't been warm all day.

We had breakfast this morning at 8 o'clock and dinner at 3 :30. We don't have but two meals today. We had a good Thanksgiving dinner consisting of mashed potatoes, chicken (imagine!), chicken dressing, gravy, salad, custard, cake, apples, cranberry sauce, syrup, hot rolls, peas, and real cream.

This evening we are going to play games.

I can't tell you how much I appreciated your box. My friends and I enjoy the food. We haven't eaten all of it yet. That cake tasted like real cake. Wouldn't I like to have some good bean soup, kraut, and onion! Oh my! I'm hungry again. Don't eat all of the kraut. Thanks again for the box.

This snow makes me think of Christmas.

Aunt Mildred! What about that? I wanted her to be valedictorian.

We had beans, bread, potatoes, and water for dinner.

I would be glad to get a few nickels if you have them. If not that is perfectly all right.

I am looking forward to seeing the twins.

We get out of school at 12 o'clock on the seventeenth of December. Try to come for us. I asked Eddie about going home with us. He said he appreciated me asking him. He said he didn't have any money. He hitchhiked down here and was leaving early hitchhiking back. I think the nearest way is by Bristol. It's farther by Norton. It will take at least twelve hours of driving. So, Daddy, start early Thursday morning, about four o'clock. You can stay all night here Friday night and rest. Then we'll start home after dinner. There isn't an extra room at the boy's dormitory. You could stay at Aunt Lou's, the woman Claude Stowers boarded with when he was down here. She wouldn't charge anything. I don't think, or not very much. She lives close here.

If you come by Bristol, you'll come by Johnson City, Tusculuan, Greenville, Morristown, Straw Plains, Knoxville, Maryville, Madisonvile, and then Hiwassee.

With Love

As you might have guessed, chicken was not as plentiful as beans and cornmeal. Thus it was much appreciated. I do not remember what I meant by real cream. However, I do remember that wild onions grew abundantly. The odor from the onions that the cows ate remained in the milk. We usually sat the pitcher of milk on the floor at one corner of the table to keep the odor of the onions away from the other food.

I had helped Mother make kraut in large stone crocks. I learned to appreciate the taste, especially the stalks of the cabbage that was trimmed and placed about in the kraut.

Mildred married my uncle, Mother's youngest brother. My uncle and I were the same age. She continued going to school and was valedictorian.

Happiness was receiving a box from home. Our looking back now, it wasn't so much what was in the box as the fact that you had received a box from home. What better time to receive a box than at Thanksgiving!

No Cooking Like Homecooking

Dec. 9, 1936

Dear Mother,

I received your letter this morning. I was very sorry to hear of Glenna's death. I always loved Glenna so much.

Tell Daddy I'm looking forward to seeing him next Thursday. Don't know for sure yet, but think two more students will come with us. They haven't definitely decided yet. I think he can count on two as far as Bluefield, Charles Sisk, a student minister from the coal fields, and another boy from Rural Retreat. Sure hope they do. It will help defray expenses.

Due to a recent rain we had muddy water to drink for four days, muddier than the creek on Clearfork ever got. The first two days I didn't drink any, then I drank it with the others. It is clear now.

They didn't wash until yesterday. So I have to begin ironing today, (Wed.).

I received a letter from Aunt Virgie. Don't have time to tell you what she said. I am sending it.

Can't think, can't study, can't work, can't write. I'm so eager to come home.

I have presents for the twins. I have made a nice one for you Mother and some things for the others.

We are still eating beans and potatoes. I want some of your homemade kraut.

Hastily,

Thursday

Just Kidding
Lib Fox

Nine more days of starvation
Then I'll be going by the station
Back to Virginia, back to civilization
The car will carry me back.

Three weeks of vacation
Then we'll leave the station
Back to Hiwassee's beans and gravy.
The bus will carry me back.

Hiwassee Journal

Jan. 26, 1936

Dear Mother,

We have been having warm rainy weather, too. It has been raining here for several days. No, we haven't had any more brown gravy. The water pipes must have been closed for awhile. Our drinking water is clear.

Have you been reading about the condition of the Ohio Valley and of Louisville, Kentucky? People are saying it is the worst disaster that has ever occurred. Many people are homeless. Hiwassee made a contribution to the people in Louisville, Kentucky. I don't know just how much.

I am sorry Grandpa isn't much better and that Grandma took the flu. I don't even have a cold but I've been taking some soda to guard against the flu.

My French teacher has the flu and my English teacher has the mumps. So, I don't have English or French this week. I am sorry they are sick, but I am glad I don't have the classes. We have a lot of work to do during the revival anyway.

Last night I saw the most interesting ball game I have ever seen. It was played in the gymn here, Hiwassee against Cumberland College from Kentucky. Cumberland College is a senior college and had never been defeated until last night. It was a close game 42-38 in favor of our boys. Our team has played several Virginia colleges and colleges from other states. They have never lost a game. What a record!

Our revivial may close tomorrow night. Here's hoping it doesn't. I honestly believe we have as good a minister as Rev. Angle. You know how much I like him. Mr. Moser, a seventy-five year old man from the "Knobs," was converted yesterday. We have two sermons a day and several prayer meetings.

It really seems like a great big family here. Rev. Kinchelo talks just as we Virginians do. So we don't get tired listening to that "lazy Southern drawl."

It is now 2:30. I began ironing just after lunch and finished all but twelve shirts. I'm going to iron them tomorrow evening.

We have the radio in the lounge fixed. I listened to the radio some this afternoon. In the city of Knoxville eleven hundred dollars were made up for the people of Louisville. Thousands of people are in distress. They were giving out distress signals and sending out motor boats.

I think I'll go visit my English teacher tomorrow, since I've already had the mumps and can't catch them anymore.

I wish you could see the flowers blooming here. There are the jonquils, the Easter Bells, the Breath of Spring, and plum trees blooming. It seems like Spring.

Evelyn, I was glad to get your letter and hear that you had won one of the debates.

Ruth, couldn't you write some, too? I don't have time to write but one letter a week. I address it to Mother, but it is meant for each of you. Will you look in my drawer and send me that piece of notebook paper that had my expenses on it? I'd like to have it down here so I'd have it all together. Thanks.

From now on I'll try to write on Wednesdays.

Tell everybody hello for me. Kiss the twins for me. Tell Phyllis Jean to make me a funny face.

Best Wishes,

Our Hiwassee Family

Feb. 2, 1937

Dear Mother and All,

Our revivial closed Sunday night. It certainly was a success. There were twenty conversions and twenty renewals. Only two girls in "our family" are not Christians. They are both orphans. It seems even more like a large family. A friendly feeling exists on our campus.

Since the revival we have had more studying to do. I had two tests today, one on English, and one on Arithmetic.

My English teacher is still sick with the mumps. Her husband gave our test to us. He said she would try to meet her classes tomorrow.

Our French teacher had the flu last week and we didn't have any classes all week. He is giving us plenty of work now. (We couldn't help it because he had the flu.)

I've already had the mumps and I don't believe I'll take the flu. I have been taking soda and eating onions. I tell Jemima, cook, every night if she doesn't let me have a big onion I might take the flu. She gives me one. I eat it just before I go to bed.

There was a meeting here yesterday of the ministers in the Sweetwater district. There were about thirty of them.

I was sorry to hear of Aunt Gladys' house burning. Wish there was something I could do for them.

I'm glad Grandpa and Grandma are feeling better. I hope the twins don't get the flu.

Mother, you need not get me any slippers now. I can make

42

these do awhile yet. They are all right. I'll write you later the kind I'd like to have.

Is it all right to give the check for nineteen dollars on this coming Saturday, Feb. 6? I'll have to pay it by then. It was due yesterday. The registrar always tells me I can have a few days to pay it. He said I could pay it Saturday.

I ironed all of my clothes this evening that weren't starched. I ironed twenty-five shirts this evening and sprinkled the starched ones to iron tomorrow. I have fifteen starched ones to iron tomorrow. I can do that in forty-five minutes, easy.

Well, we just have one more month of this quarter, and then one more quarter, (three months). Next month we begin the last quarter of this school year. I will have to buy some new books then. I will be taking Political Science, Public School Music, and Art. I believe I will really like these subjects. I think it will be possible to get second-hand books except for Art. You have to have new Art supplies such as crayons, etc. I am going to get my books with another girl so they won't cost too much. I'll write later exactly how much they will cost. I don't know for sure now.

No, the flood didn't reach us. We have that to be thankful for.

I received a long letter from Bert. It was full of news and so cheery. I had written her that I smelled the beans burning. She said she was going to mail me a box. My hints are usually every effective, aren't they? I try to write her once in awhile and home once every week. That's all the writing I'm doing. I am studying hard and don't have much time.

Did I tell you that I received a pretty calendar from the Bland Bank? I have a calendar from Luther's store hanging in my room. Several girls asked me if my father had a store.

Think I'm getting the flu.

With love,

Some people believed that a teaspoon of soda taken in a half glass of water would keep the flu away, They also believed that onion eaten would keep the flu bug away. At this time I, too, must have believed in its magic. Later I took the flu and ran a high temperature for a few days. The lounge was made into an infirmary.

All Kind of Things

Hello Mother, Daddy, Ruth W. H., Evelyn, Bud and the Twins,

I'm so sorry all of you had the flu. I'm better now. I didn't miss much in school, for my teachers were sick part of the time. I'm attending all of my classes now.

My ironing is finished. I, also, helped another girl so she could hold her job. I hope the girl is back by next week and I feel she will be. Mrs. Kirkland, supervisor in the laundry, helped me some this week. I thought that was very sweet of her.

I didn't get your letter until Wednesday, I always look for one on Tuesdays. I thought probably it had lain over at the post office. Then I got it this morning.

Having noticed that the letter I received when I was sick was postmarked a week ahead, I wondered if this was the latest thing.

I'm sorry Aunt Susie is so sick. I wish I had seen her when I was in at Christmas time.

I'm glad you haven't sent me a box, because my roommate has been in bed seriously ill since last Monday. She has the mumps on both sides. She is better now. I'm glad I've already had them. She is better now and is beginning to eat solid food. I think by next week she could help me enjoy a box.

Exams begin next week. Then the next Monday we register again for the last quarter.

Seems like school is almost out. I just have one more quarter to go this year. I wrote you the subjects I was taking this quarter. For last month's grade I made on English B, French B, Penmanship A, and Arithmetic B. This quarter's grades will soon be in.

I was glad to get the statement, the card from Bud, and especially glad to get the valentines from the twins. I'd like to see the little sweet things.

We're going to have applesauce for supper. I saw Jemima throwing out the cans. There's the bell.

All my love,

Our room was over the dining hall, across from the shower. It was larger than most of the rooms and a bit more private because of its location. It was sometimes called Devil's Den or Angel's Rest according to the behavior of its occupants. We could look down at the kitchen door and know what we were having for dinner. I never remember any menus being posted. This is why I meant by watching Jemima throwing away the cans.

Virginia Club

My Dearest Mother and all,

It's only about ten minutes until supper time — *5:30.* It will be 6:30 up there. Maybe you are eating supper.

I was a little disappointed when your letter didn't come this morning. It came in the evening mail.

No. You didn't write me about Aunt Susie being in the hospital.

After supper:

We had beans, sweet potatoes, and applesauce for supper.

Yes, I received my slippers. They were a perfect fit. I wore them once and like them fine. I am keeping them new for Easter.

Our Easter services begin this Sunday and last a week. We will have several plays and new speakers. On Easter morning we will have a communion service. I am told that it is a big event.

I still like my subjects fine. We had a music test the other day on the keys and notes. I made 100 on it. I really like Art. We haven't got our supplies yet. They will probably be here by tomorrow. We have already made a sand table with Robinson Crusoe's island on it, put up borders on board and made window decorations. It doesn't require much study but plenty of time and imagination. I love it!

The work I did in Miss Crabtree's Art class last year was a

good beginning. I'm getting along all right in English and in Political Science, too. Political Science is almost like the Government class I had under Mr. Reynolds last year. So I have a good foundation for it.

I like my course better than either of the other two quarters. I'm going to try to get an A on Music and Art anyway. I want to have better grades this quarter than the other two quarters. Have you received my grades for last quarter yet? They are English B, Management C-plus, Penmanship A, Arithmetic B, and French B. This gives me an average of 90 for the second quarter. This is a little lower than the first quarter. However I carried 18 hours and only 15 hours the first quarter. Then I missed a week when I had the flu. That was hard to make up. I believe the subjects I took last quarter were harder for me than these I'm taking now. My average for next quarter should be higher. I will try to make it so. When I missed with the flu, I missed going to church one Sunday. Thus, I didn't get an additional three points added to my grades as I did last quarter.

It is about 6 o'clock. We have Life Service Band at 7 o'clock.

I'm on the program committee of the Virginia Club. We meet in a few minutes to give out parts for our program. We plan to do three stunts and include every member in it. We are not giving the play we meant to give since we could not locate a book. We are using the state song, Carry Me Back To Old Virginia. Mother Helvey will play it for us.

The stamps were appreciated as well as both of the letters. Tell Ruth to write me when she has time. Ask Ruth and Evelyn if they plan to enter the contests at the end of school. By all means, one of them should enter. "Keep up your good grades. I want to see one of you as valedictorian. That isn't asking too much, is it?"

Daddy, I hope that will help some, not paying until May. I realize that it is a real sacrifice on the part of you and Mother in keeping me down here. I feel that the least I can do now to repay you both is to make the best grades I can and get the most worthwhile things I can get here. Then I can pay the money back when I teach. It doesn't seem a very long time. I can teach in the fall of 1938.

Do you remember the boy who came back to Richlands with us at Christmas time? He finished last quarter. I suppose he will teach next year.

How's the plowing coming along?

Tell the twins, "Hi."

Don't you or Mother work too hard.

I, thoroughly, enjoy my work here.

I am looking forward to cooking your supper and making you some custard pies. I haven't cooked anything for so long, though.

It is doubtful whether you'll be able to eat it or not.

I must go to service now.

Love to all,
Your daughter

More than anything else except my mother's homemade lightbread my father loved custard pies. I had learned to bake them when I was very young. We had plenty of milk and eggs on the farm. These were the main ingredients in a custard pie.

I was concerned that Daddy and Mother were sacrificing so much in order to pay for my education.

My sister, Ruth, was valedictorian of her high school that year, with Evelyn as co-salutorian. I had every right to be proud of both of them. Ruth later graduated from West Virginia Business College. She is presently employed at Bassett Printing Corporation, Bassett, Va. Evelyn attended and graduated from Hiwassee College. She became a teacher for one year and an airline stewardess for eight years. She now lives in Poway, California.

Life Service Band was later named Christian Worker's Council.

Memorial Service

My Dearest Mother,

I usually take a nap on Sunday evening, but I didn't today. The college held a memorial service for four boys who were students here and had recently passed away. In their memory a tablet of marble was unveiled which had their names engraved upon it. There were four white candles burning. Then there was a wheel covered in white paper with four spokes cut short and the hub. The minister said the four spokes represented the boys, and the hub represented Christ. One of the boys lived in West Virginia in the coal mining area of Jenkins Jones. Several of his relatives attended. The service began about 2 o'clock and lasted an hour.

During the last week we had several distinguished speakers from Kentucky and near-by cities. Enjoyed the talks so much.

This morning the auditorium, (we use it as church) was decorated with peach blossoms and Regal lilies. Also the different classrooms were decorated. Tonight Mrs. Colston is giving an Easter play. This ends the services for Holy Week.

How many eggs did you eat? We had a boiled one apiece for breakfast. We had an unusually nice dinner and a colored egg. I got a green one. We are getting another boiled one in our "hand-outs" tonight for supper. I guess the twins ate my eggs. I hope all of you had a nice Easter.

Just two more months of school. I found out what I made on English this month, but I haven't found out what I made on anything else. I made 93 on English. I'm sure I did better on Art and Music. Have you received my grades for the last quarter? I wrote you what they were but I wondered if the registrar had mailed them to you.

Well, I've told you all that's happened. I'll finish writing Wednesday.

Tuesday night

Your letter received this morning. I enjoyed it so much. No, I wasn't disappointed because I didn't get a dress. I wore my pink blouse and pressed my blue skirt and wore it. That looked nice. I enjoyed the service just as much as if I had been all dressed up. It isn't the clothes that make a person anyway. Is it? That's what you always told us.

I will appreciate the boxes, of course. They are always appreciated. I enjoyed that little hand print of Phyllis Jean's. It was so cute. Mother, I believed I enjoyed it nearly as much as I did your letter.

Oh yes, we had a nice dinner Easter; pork chops, gravy, peas, macaroni, gelatin salad, colored egg, and cake. But I would have enjoyed the food you had more.

Mrs. Allen promised me a start of her orange sultana, and I think I am going to get a pretty begonia to bring back with me.

I still like my subjects. I, yet, do not know my Art and Music grades, but know they are all right.

The Castalian Literary Society, (not ours) is going to give a play tonight entitled, Spooky Tavern. Admission is free. I want to see

Just two more months and I'll get to see those sweet little twins.

Love to all,

P. S. Phyllis Jean likes onions, for she takes that after her sis.

It was a custom at Easter to see how many eggs we could eat. For a few days before Easter we would hide the eggs. My favorite place for hiding was in the binder where the ball of twine was kept. I would take out the twine and fill the container with eggs. I could easily hide two or three dozen there.

"Handouts", as we called them, were bag lunches given out on Sunday evenings. They usually consisted of a peanut-jelly sandwich, tuna fish salad sandwich, and a piece of fruit.

Little things in life still mean so much, just as did the small handprint of a little sister.

Mother collected flower clippings of all kinds. I knew the flowers would make her happy.

Love For Hiwassee

May 2, 1937

Dearest Mother and all,

Perhaps you have heard from me by now. I mailed you a Mother's Day card and a letter on Thursday. I was thinking that Mother's Day was this Sunday. It isn't until May 9th. I was sure you would get the letter this week. It must have been misplaced.

Yes, I'm as well as can be. My cold is better. I hope you are feeling fine. I'll be glad to come home so I can help with the work.

It is raining here now. I had planned to go for a short walk, but since it is raining I will have to stay in.

The trees on the campus are beautiful. The dogwood near the campus is getting old. Seems like we have a lot of rain.

I will get out of school on the twenty-fifth of May. I would rather come home on the train, if you want me to. It won't be any higher, about the same as the bus. I think all of the Virginia bunch are going by train. If I do this, I will come a new way through the edge of Kentucky and by Norton, Virginia. I'd rather do this since I've seen the places where the bus passes. Write me which you think I should do. I can be in Norton at 10:30 on the twenty-sixth, leaving here at night. Daddy could ask about what time the train leaving after 10:30 from Norton to Bluefield arrives. Then he could meet the train at that time. I could be home on the night of the twenty-sixth. In going from here to Bluefield by-bus, I'd have to wait over at Knoxville and Bristol, too. Thus, I could make about as good time and see several new places.

Next Sunday we have a Mother's Day program, the next Sunday a regular sermon, then the next Sunday the baccalaureate sermon.

Is Bert planning to come down the last of school? I wish she'd wait and come next year to see me graduate. Of course, that's up to her. I can see why she'd like to come back. I don't believe anyone could get far enough away to stop loving Hiwassee. It's like living on a big farm and that's just about what it is. Everyone has his own work to do and enjoys it.

It is still raining. I am wondering what each of you are doing. It won't be long until I see you. Think I'll take me a nap.

Lots of love,

Written in the back of my Bible I studied at Hiwassee are these words, telling how the environment influenced me during my stay there: "It seems to me that a good way of estimating how much a thing is really worth is to think how much we would have missed had we not had that thing. When I tried to think of my life without Hiwassee it seemed that something was left out, that something valuable was missing. I know I am much stronger spiritually for having been here now almost two years. I shall always remember Hiwassee as a place where clean living and fellowship predominate."

Second Year

Sept. 21, 1937

Dearest Mother and all,

I was glad to receive your letter this morning. Thanks for sending the check also. I'll not need any more money until nineteen dollars next month.

I'm glad the kids like going to school. I enjoy school a lot, especially Practice Teaching and History. I never did like History until this year. Our teacher makes it come alive.

I can't believe the teachers are getting sixty dollars per month. It seems impossible. I'm certainly glad to hear it.

I thought of Daddy's birthday being Monday. Had I been there I would have greased his nose.

I like my hose fine. They are nice.

Yesterday I taught to make up for Thursday, election day. The election is held at the schoolhouse.

Wish you could go to conference. Our pastor, Rev. Abshire, will be there and perhaps speak. He's a grand pastor.

Yesterday, Monday, Jemima and I set out some flowers. I helped her reset some. She gave me the prettiest fern you ever saw. I have it setting in front of one of the windows and it almost covers it. Besides that I have some Wandering Jew, Sultanas, Coleus, and a Snake Plant started. They are growing pretty. The room looks nice.

Have had several compliments on my kimona you made me.

One girl is paying me by the month to keep her hair fixed.

Mother Helvey has a bad finger. For awhile I thought she might lose it. She ran a needle in it and it got infected. It is better now.

My ironing is finished. Have a test on History today.

I'm chairman of the committee that plans the programs for prayer meeting. Our subject this week is Cut Your Goods By His Pattern. You know how I like to sew.

Just before supper:

1 didn't have time to finish the letter before dinner and have been busy this evening helping plan programs and taking Physical Education. In Physical Education we are playing tennis. There are only four in this class. I don't know much about it yet, but I like to play.

It is almost supper time. We are having cheese and crackers for supper.

My books are paid for. Thanks for money.

Tell Phyllis Jean, Barbara Dean, and Donald, Hello.

Best wishes,
Your daughter

Mother had taken some small silk scraps of different sizes of fabric and pieced them together, just as they were. Then out of the fabric she made a kimona or robe. After she finished she embroidered a cross stitch over each seam. No one else in the dormitory had a robe just like mine. It was beautiful! I wore it for years afterwards. It would be very much in style today with so much patchwork being worn.

Practice Teaching

Sept. 28, 1937

Dearest Mother and all,

Your letter was enjoyed very much.

It is beginning to be cool here. The leaves are beginning to turn.

I asked Dr. Frick, our new president, about paying the first of November. He said that would be all right and that he was glad he could help me. He said he had received a letter from Rev. Angle asking about me.

Yes, I still like Practice Teaching very much. Today we were sent out into the Smokies to teach some older people who could neither read nor write. It is part of our work. It was my job to visit and try to help a man who is in his seventies. I wondered what I would talk about. We began talking about his mountain farm. I enjoyed the visit, but it is not as exciting to me as working with children. We will be going once each week. I am not hopeful of teaching him very much, but I shall try to brighten his day. He is not well and seemed to enjoy my visit.

I can't help but wonder what grades I'll make this first month. I had History test this morning. Think I did very well on it.

I don't know how many pupils are here this year, probably about three hundred. There is talk of making this a four year college in the future. Several questions concerning the college will be decided at conference. I hope you can be there.

Yes, I stay busy most of the time. It takes a lot of time to study.

I'm enjoying choir practice a lot. I have learned several new songs.

Mother Helvey's finger is better. I was worried about it for awhile.

Where is Glorena teaching?

I would love to see the .twins and Donald. I bet they have grown a lot since I left.

I must stop and go to the library.

Love,

I did, indeed, like student teaching. However, I can remember coming to the cooperating teacher with a feeling of insecurity and uncertainty; even though I had had previous experience in working with young people. I felt anxious and wanted someone to tell me what to do. Now I realize that anxiety is a natural reaction whenever a person is starting a new job. I soon realized that it was the desire of both the principal and the cooperating teacher for my experience to be a successful one.

Since that time I have been a cooperating teacher and have observed student teachers as they gain in confidence and poise.

Halloween Pranks

Nov. 2, 1937

Dearest Mother and all,

I received your letter this morning just before History class. I didn't read it until History was over, because I thought I'd have a test on History. Imagine me waiting that long! Then I didn't have a test.

It is a pretty day here, almost like a Spring day.

You wrote about the bridge being broken. That makes me think of the time Daddy had when he went after the batteries. The other day I wrote a paper on that. It was so funny! I made 93 on it.

Quite a few pranks were pulled here, too. Sunday morning when we got up we saw an old wagon in front of the dining room steps, a mule on the campus, some fodder, and a cow in the boy's shower room.

I'll give the check tomorrow or the next day. Write me when I can give the remainder.

All of the seniors who expect to graduate this Spring are supposed to see Mr. Youell this week. He checks to see if you have the right requirements. I have already talked with him and found exactly what I'll be taking the next two quarters. Winter quarter: Bible, History, Geography and Practice Teaching. Spring quarter: Bible, Zoology, Child Psychology, Children's Literature, and Physical Education. I will have one hundred hours when I graduate. Only ninety- six are required.

I had three more pupils this morning in fourth grade English. That makes twenty-two in English and six in Reading.

I had a nice letter from Bert. I answered it yesterday.

It's about time to get ready for Physical Education.

Tell the twins and Donald, Hello.

Write all the news.

With love to all,

I have a different job. Really, I don't mind being the janitor! One thing about it, since I'm janitor I'm going to be the best janitor I know how to be.

The curtains in the three bathrooms have been hanging for so long that they look bedraggled and needed washing. I took them down, cleaned the windows, and attempted to hand wash them. They came to shreds. I told Mother Halvey if I had some fabric I could make curtains for windows, by hand. The fabric, a thin grade of muslin, was supplied. The curtains were made and hung. How nice they look! I made a few extra trips to the bathroom to admire them.

Love,

What joy it is to do a job well whether it be a cake straight from the oven, a quilt just quilted, a dress made, or a yard trimmed. I still stand back and admire my work. I seem to hear my father say, "Do the best you can, try to keep up with the plow."

I try to teach boys and girls not to be satisfied with their work, unless it's the best they can do.

Attends Teacher's Meeting

Nov. 7, 1937

Dearest Mother and all,

We surely have been busy the last few days. The pupils of the training school are giving a play up here Tuesday night. Each practice teacher has had to train one pupil.

Miss Bryson took a few girls with her yesterday to the teachers meeting at Madisonville. I went from the training school and others went from the high school. Did we feel important at a real teacher's meeting! We heard the best talk given by the state supervisor of Tennessee. I took notes on it. When we got back we gave a report telling what we saw and heard.

The other morning a missionary from Knoxville, who had been around the world, talked to us and showed us idols that were worshipped by other peoples and costumes from different countries. I wish you could have heard the talk. It was well worth the listening. She talked about three hours to us.

Monday Morning:

I am cleaning bathrooms now. I have three bathrooms and one shower. This is easier than ironing. I clean them each day. Today I have cleaned them and studied some.

We had a good time yesterday. Some of our pupils brought us some turnips and peanuts to bring home with us. The turnips are so good.

Mother, if you can find it, please send me one of the price lists to the hosiery company. I thought I could get up an order and get me a free pair.

My books next quarter will cost three dollars and fifty cents, getting them second-hand and with someone else. The next quarter begins on the thirtieth of this month.

The coat fits all right. The candy was good.

Tuesday night:

I was a little disappointed when I didn't get a letter this morning, but thought perhaps you had missed the mail. I got it a few minutes ago in the evening mail. So glad to get it.

I hope you didn't misunderstand me when I said I had to wait until History was over to read your last letter. It wasn't because I wanted to. It was almost History time when I got the letter and I couldn't manage to read it in class, although I wanted to read it and was hoping the teacher would be called out of the room.

I am eager to see the new cellar Daddy built for us.

We get out of school on Dec. 18. That shouldn't be so long.

Sorry you have had colds. I haven't had the slightest cold.

You might send me a quarter sometime to have the heel taps put on my white slippers. I lost the taps and don't like to wear my black ones every day.

The registrar announced this morning that all accounts must be settled by the 18th of the month before we would be allowed to take our examinations. I am eight dollars behind.

Yes, we will have school on Armistice Day. We will have a few days for Thanksgiving.

My flowers look very pretty. I moved them over by the windows where they could get lots of sunshine.

I'm a bit tired. I've been helping fix the stage for a play and playing tennis.

Mother Helvey is all right and just as sweet and good as ever.

Tell everybody Hi. I'd like to peep in now and see what

Donald, P. J., and B. D. are doing.

Lots of love,

Daddy had built a cellar in the side of the hill behind the house. It was made of rock and had an apple house overhead. In the cellar were kept half-gallon and quart size cans of food to be used in the winter. There were cans of all kinds of food, especially huckleberries, picked on Big Ridge, and grape juice made from the grapes on the farm. Many bushels of apples and potatoes were also stored for the winter season. I can remember him showing me the potato sprouts in the dark cellar and telling me there was a lesson there. For they always grew toward the light.

Applies For School

Dearest Mother and all,

Is it cold up there? We had a little snow this morning. It soon melted.

I wonder what you are doing this evening.

I'm in bed trying to keep warm. The heat is beginning to come on and the room is getting warmer. We have the warmest room in the hail.

All of my exams are over. It feels good not to have to study for awhile. However, I'm sure I'll get tired of resting and will be ready to study the next quarter. I only had to take two exams. I made 96 on Hygiene and I know I made equally as well on History. I made A on Practice Teaching. I was happy. I'd rather have an A on that than anything.

I wrote Mr. Stowers a letter asking for a school in his district. I also wrote Mr. Robinette. I had the librarian type my letters and mailed them this morning. I enclosed a stamped envelope in each one and will expect an answer soon.

Thanks for the money to get my shoes. I ordered me a brown pair. I needed them. The soles of mine are getting thin. I use my tennis shoes for hiking and playing tennis.

Last Sunday afternoon a group of us walked eight miles to church. I wish I could write you all about it but I couldn't tell you about it in a whole letter. The church was a log house, not nearly as good as the old shop that used to be across the creek.

For seats we had boards nailed to stumps. I sat down in front of what had been a fireplace. The fireplace had been covered with cardboard. I was afraid to lean backward.

Now that I have plenty of time I can't remember what I've written and what I haven't.

Did I write you about seeing the Indians? Eight of them came here from Red Rock, Oklahoma and presented a program to the school. They were real Indians from a reservation. Chief Treewater, the chief of the tribe, gave a talk. Then they did some war dances and told about their customs. The chief had black hair plaited in two braids. This was interesting.

Many of the students will be going home for Thanksgiving. One of the girls asked me to keep her radio for her.

I have been giving quite a few finger waves. There was a football banquet last night. I gave seven waves and a shampoo. I waved Mother Helvey's hair, too, yesterday. Of course, I never get that much business on an ordinary day. I've been making enough money to buy paper, pencils, soap, etc. I think that helps some and I like to do it. I may make a little money over the holidays. I doubt it though, for so many will be going home.

Dr. Frick gave us an interesting talk this morning.

Miss Bryson has asked me to give an exam for her tomorrow. She has the questions all made out.

Must mail this.

Love to all,

It was an exciting time. I had worked and waited for a long time to send in an application for a position as a teacher in Bland County, Va. I could hardly wait until the reply came back.

Waiting Tables

Dearest Mother, W. H., Bud and all,

Enjoyed all of your letters. I have just finished taking a test in Bible. I think I did all right on it.

Well, my tooth doesn't hurt now. I went with Mother Helvey Thursday and had it pulled. Write me when I can pay the dollar. I'd like to do it this week if I can. Mother Helvey was so nice and didn't charge me anything for taking me to Madisonville.

I don't guess I'll have to pay for my invitations before the first of the quarter. That will be about a dollar and I'll have to buy books then, too.

Just one more week and this quarter will be up. Then three more months!

I'll get my books as cheap as I can. I don't know exactly what they will cost. Maybe I'll know by next week.

I am waiting tables now. I like to do it. I have learned a lot.

We have been having some pretty weather here. Today it is rainy. It seems like Spring.

I have attended a few basketball games in the last few weeks. Hiwassee has won the majority of them, only lost a time or two.

Glad you made good grades, Bud. You must study hard. The other day I said to one of my pupils, "Maybe I'm not giving the class enough work to do." She seemed to think I was giving them enough to do. I try to see that they work and work hard.

I smell BEANS cooking, beans and cornbread. That's good though, isn't it?

Love to twins, Donald and all,

Waiting tables was another experience for me. I had three tables. I got up early, went down to the dining hall, set the tables and placed the food on the tables. If I hurried I could get seconds for my tables. The students really appreciated a waitress who could get seconds. We stood in line for seconds. Then afterwards the table had to be cleared and the dishes carried back to the kitchen.

Attends Banquet

Dearest Mother and all,

Have you received my quarter grades yet? I made A on Bible and A on History for the quarter. I didn't know this when I wrote you the last letter.

I have all of my books except one. I had to have a laboratory manual in Zoology. It cost one dollar and forty cents. I asked my teacher to order one for me. This is the first year Zoology has been taught here. I am the only girl from the dormitory taking the class. There are a few day students in the class.

I paid for my invitations and have enough money for the manual. I may need a little money later on for my picture in the annual. I don't know yet.

Zoology is hard. It is a study of animals. I shall study hard. I think it will be more interesting later. We will begin lab. work tomorrow. Later we will cut up a cat, pigeon, turtle, dogfish, and snake. Imagine me doing that. I bet I could cut up a turtle. I have watched while you cut up a turtle.

Old Testament Bible isn't hard but Rev. Abshire certainly can keep you busy.

Rev, and Mrs. Abshire gave the choir a banquet last night at 7:30 in the dining hall. It was informal. I wore my blue dress, that one of Ruth's. It looked nice. We had a good time.

We had some singing and a talk by the choir director. Plans were made for Easter music. The choir is going in a truck Easter morning to Madisonville about two hours before daybreak and sing Easter carols up or down every street until breakfast time. We have learned so many new songs. The director seems to be pleased with the choir. We have a better one than we had last year. We practice twice a week. We might get to sing somewhere soon, perhaps Sweetwater.

Yes, I'll have plenty of time to get some clothes in May.

Think I'd like to encourage all of the old maids to get married so there will be some vacancies next year. Bedtime now.

Love,

I was offered a position at Grapefield, Va. Needless to say I was overjoyed. Salary was to be sixty-five dollars per month. Later I learned that I had forty-five pupils and grades one through seven. I enjoyed my pupils and did everything with them except play football. Home visitation was no problem. It was expected that the teacher spend at least one night at the home of each pupil. This I did. There was no janitorial service. Fires also had to be kept going in the winter. Water was carried from a well. The school day began at nine o'clock and lasted until four o'clock.

Works In Kitchen

Tuesday morning

Dearest Mother and all,

I was surprised getting the dress. It is a perfect fit. Ruby and I were talking the day before about what colors we liked. I said lavender. She said I couldn't wear it until Easter. I haven't worn it until today.

We are not having classes today. Our pictures are being taken for the annual. I have paid for all of mine except engraving fee of one dollar ($1.00). The first of the month will be early enough for that. I thought about not having my pictures in the annual. I decided that I would since I was a senior. The annual will be nicer than the one last year. I will have my picture in the Christian Worker's Council, Philomathesian Literary Society, Virginia Club, Choir, individual picture, and maybe as waitress in the dining hall.

Jemina has been sick. I have been helping in the kitchen.

Ruby and I picked enough water cress yesterday for her, Jemima, and my supper. Was it good!

Ruby and I have a new room-mate, Nannie Lou Kidd, from Maryville, Tennessee. I like her as much as I like Ruby, so you know she's sweet. She has taught school and is older than we are. There are three in most all of the rooms now. You've heard me talk about Nancy. It's the same girl.

Today looks like Spring, so pretty outside.

I need a pair of hose. Mine are wearing out. Waiting tables is hard on hose.

Tell the twins and Donnie, Hello.

How will I remember the lavender-flowered dress. I wore it for my picture for the annual, 1938.

Nannie Lou Kidd (Nancy) married Frank Simerly and lives at Friendsville, Tennessee. We have continued our friendship by correspondence since 1938.

Gathers Watercress

10:20

Dearest Mother and all,

Glad to get your letter and Evelyn's.

You said in your letter you wondered what I was doing. Ruby and I were just getting in from a long walk, about four o'clock, five o'clock up there. We went for a walk, just after lunch, visited a woman who lived way out in the woods. We got a box from her and brought it back full of watercress and a bag of walnuts.

Left to right: Nancy Kidd, Josie Philpot and Ruby Cox with a box of water cress and a bag of walnuts.

We brought back at least a peck of walnuts. She told us to help ourselves. They were out under the trees, ten bushels I guess in all and as dry as dry could be. We put the water cress in the refrigerator and had it for supper last night. We gave Jemima and Doc a bowl full and we ate the remainder. Good! Have you had a "mess~~ yet?

My flowers are very pretty. I have another begonia started that Jemima gave me. It is an Angel Wing, I believe.

I'm glad Donald is getting along all right. I bet he has grown a lot. Ruby and I saw a little baby Sunday, eight months old.

Thanks for the hose. I hated to write for them, but I needed them. No, I don't need any slippers now. I think I can make these until commencement time. I wear my tennis shoes on hikes. We go out into the mountains and hold Sunday School on Sundays. We walk eight miles each Sunday.

Rev. Abshire's wife is in the hospital. We are not having Bible but have plenty of outside work on Abraham, Jacob, Isaac, Joseph, and Moses's lives.

After lunch:

Sorry you didn't get to enter the reading contest.

Yes, Nancy is still rooming with us. We like her a lot.

We've had a little shower this evening. Everything looks pretty. The grass is so green.

Hi P. J. and B. D.

Love to all,

The twins were babies when I left to go to college, being born in 1935. Donald was born in 1937. This accounts for their names being mentioned so many times.

I can remember hearing Daddy say to us, "You must help your mother all you can. She isn't feeling very well." I knew she was pregnant. I helped carry water so that she didn't have to lift heavy loads.

Donald was born in the summer before I went back to Hiwassee for the second year. I remember being kidded. I was a senior in college and I had a baby brother.

Quilting Bee

My Dearest Mother,

Yes, I was surprised when I saw Ruth's essay in the paper. Nancy, Ruby, Annie Ruth, and I had started over to Mrs. Brunner's to a quilting bee when I got the paper. I opened the paper and was thrilled to see that she had won the contest.

Mrs. Brunner put us to quilting on a Flower Garden quilt. You know how slow they are to quilt. I quilted a square and a half.

I know I couldn't have earned my dinner. We had the best dinner; fried chicken, gravy, green beans, meat, pudding, sweet potatoes with walnuts, tea, and butterscotch pie. It did us good to get something different to eat.

Mrs. Brunner gave me a new quilt pattern, flower basket.

It won't be long until graduation. I hope Daddy, Ruth and Bert can come down then. They'll enjoy it.

I must study Zoology.

Tell twins and Donnie, Hi.

Love,

Quilting always appealed to me. When I was a young child Mother would have quiltings. The quilt would be ready for quilting, hanging from the ceiling. About six of the neighbor ladies would get around the frame and quilt while three or four ladies cooked in the kitchen. Such a meal! Sometimes if they started early in the morning they would finish the quilt that day.

Sometimes they came back and finished it the next day. I often believed that Mother had a way of putting the best cooks in the kitchen, and the best quilters at the quilting frames. I had watched Mother and quilted some, so I knew how it was done. I also knew the names of many quilt patterns, such as Tree of Life, Dutch Girl, Lone Star, Flower Garden and Rose of Sharon.

Learn, Laugh, Love, Lift

On Tuesday morning, May 24, 1938, 10:30 a.m. eighty-five students graduated from Hiwassee College. The graduation exercises began with a processional followed by a literary address. Dean Youell awarded the diplomas. I was one of those receiving a diploma. My name was called out as one who had made one of the highest averages.

My father and sister, Ruth, were present for the occasion. They had come down for my graduation and to take me home.

It was good to be back on the farm.

That fall the training I had had as janitor in college proved to be valuable. In my first contract was written these words, "School room to be kept clean by teacher."

For the next few years my pupils and I sat around a pot-bellied stove and tried to keep warm.

Wood was sold by cords. The county paid for a certain number of cords of wood. The lowest bidder got the job of furnishing the wood for the school. I remember one year the man who got the job brought green sycamore. All it did was sputter. Had my father not brought me some slabs of wood to mix with the sycamore I think we would have frozen.

Now it is impossible for me to enter the building where I teach without being grateful for a warm building with plenty of supplies.

With the help of some of my older pupils I whitewashed one room where I taught.

Cafeterias were unheard of at that time in country schools. On Friday the pupils and I brought the ingredients and made hot chocolate. Other Fridays we had boiled eggs. The eggs boiled while we sat around the stove and tried to keep warm. Another time we boiled potatoes. These delicacies were a welcome addition to our cold lunches.

I had one more grandmother who wasn't my grandmother.

Grandma King and her husband.

She was an old lady who lived about a block above a little one-room school where I taught. Her name was Mrs. King. I called her Grandma King and thought of her as such. She had been able to write but her hands were crippled with arthritis. On bad days I stayed at her house instead of wading mud and snow. When she wanted me to come up and answer her letters she'd put a red bandana handkerchief in a peach tree for a flag. I'd look to see if the bandana was there. If it was I'd go up and answer her letters.

Stowersville School. I taught here when I was answering letters for Grandma King. This was also where the room was whitewashed.

I have found children to be delightful and very unpredictable. A few years ago one of my fifth grade boys was reading a selection from the Bible, Psalms 16, King James Version. The verse starts by David saying, "Oh God, thou hast cast us off." The boy read, "Oh God, thou has cussed us out!"

Later I was trying to get across the idea of the importance of being accurate in measuring and counting. I asked the class to think of an example at school where counting incorrectly would make a difference. I said, "Suppose we sent the lunch count in as fifty instead of twenty-five. What difference would that make? I expected the answer to be a waste of food and money.

Instead I got the answer, "We'd all get seconds." The rewards are many!

By the time I have finished this writing I will have taught a quarter of a century. It is my belief that knowledge and preparation are important assets to a teacher, but I believe one of the most important characteristics a teacher can possess is a genuine love for children.

Some of the sayings or stories that have given me values that I try to live by are: Always go the second mile. Grandpa's story of sticking together, Daddy's story of keeping up with the plow, Daddy's example of heaping it up and running it over, Do the best you can, and "Honesty is the best policy."

One day I picked up two bank envelopes out of the holder on the outside of the bank. I took them home and laid them in my desk. Later when I picked up one of the envelopes to deposit my check, I noticed that one envelope had some money in it. The person had put the money in the wrong place. I didn't have to think what to do. I took the envelope and money back to the bank and told the clerk where I had found it. I could almost hear my parents say, "Honesty is the best policy."

I have not thought of the story as spending my time looking regretfully backwards. Some of what you found here may make you glad you live in this modern day. It is hard to visualize the trials of yesteryear from today's conveniences. However, as we live in today's society we have a tendency to forget that everything we have was made possible by our ancestors. I believe we need an awareness of this heritage and growth.

Part Two
Short Stories

I Remember Daddy

By: Beulah S. Fox, Copyright 1988   Reprinted from Mountain Laurel, October, 1988

My father was Wiley Hicks Stowers (1891-1955). If someone were to ask me what things I remember most about my father, I would say his honesty, integrity, and generosity.

I was the oldest of eight children and I would go with him to deliver produce. We'd get up about three in the morning and leave home to go to Bluefield, Virginia, and West Virginia to deliver produce, which had been loaded the night before on a spring wagon.

When we arrived Daddy would stop the wagon half way up the hollow and the customers would come running. He'd fill a bushel basket to the top and then keep filling until its contents ran over, saying the Bible always said to give good measure and running over. He was a Christian who lived the Bible every day of the week, having been church school superintendent for twenty-seven years. Each Christmas, somehow, he managed to treat each child with candies and oranges, paying for them himself.

Since I was the oldest I helped him hang gates, dig post holes, and mend fences. When spring came he turned the sod and made even rows in the fresh soil. Later my sister, brother and I hoed corn. He'd tell us, "Try and keep up with the plow."

Hicks got the shortest row, Ruth got the next shortest and I got the longest row, according to the age and ability. These lessons and others have stayed with me.

Memories leapfrog through my mind now as I gaze at his dinner pail with a wire handle and a tin cup that fits on top. At noon Mother would bring it to the field. It had biscuits and vegetables in the bottom, fried apple pies in the tray, along with a gallon of milk, cold from the spring in a White House vinegar jar. We ate beneath the poplar trees scattered with yellow tulips that cast lacy shadows in the corner of the rail fence.

For a while we were free to talk while muscles relaxed, to dream of going swimming, fishing, playing house, or exploring the cave. He knew where the biggest blackberries grew and would show us where to find them. Two of the things he didn't like were canned tomatoes and cornbread. He loved custard pies.

One crisp fall morning, I went with my father to the back field in the edge of the mountain to shuck corn. He had made me a little corn shucker that fit my hand. I was trying to work fast so my fingers would keep warm, when on the other side of the shock I heard a noise. A mother deer was eating corn. I wondered how we would gain if we worked and the deer ate. I thought we might gain some since there were two of us and only one deer. Daddy saw the deer and said, " Be quiet, let her eat." After she ate a while she walked away.

On rainy days he'd work in the shop. Always he'd say, "Put things where you found them". He remembered exactly how the tools were lying, if pointed in one direction he expected them to point in the same direction. Daddy had a different sense of humor from most people. He was building a rock foundation for our porch. While doing this he found a rock on the farm with a lump sticking outward, calling it a pregnant rock. Today the rock is still cemented in the foundation reminding me of him. He did his own carpenter work and always said you could cover a multitude of sins with corner round, meaning if something didn't exactly fit you could remedy it. A real problem existed that he never overcame. If there was something in the road he was sure to hit it. It didn't matter so much when he was driving a team of horses because Maud and Nell were skillful in dodging the bumps and holes in the road.

One day Daddy went to Bland and bought a car. We saw the dealer and him go up the road – the dealer was driving. After a few minutes the car came down the road and Daddy was driving. This was the only lesson he ever had, about a half mile's worth. Being accustomed to working with horses, he didn't realize he had the engine power of many horses at his fingertips. He'd talk to the car like he was talking to a team of horses.

It was a while before any of the family would ride with him. Then one day he loaded us into the car and we were on our way to church. We children didn't help any. When another car was approaching, Bud would say, "Hit him and run Daddy, hit him and run." He was the youngest at the time and had been used to playing with toy cars and bumping them together. Hicks would say, "Put the bridle on him". Another would say, "Can't you slow down?" While another would say, "Can't you go faster than that?" In the winter the road was frozen into deep ruts, mud holes in wet weather and clouds of dust when it was dry. Somehow he managed, having only one wreck on a foggy morning.

These things speak softly of a part of my life. I'm glad I had him for a dad, for he surely left a lot of tracks.

A Strange Animal

It was hot that day and Daddy was thirsty. He told me to bring a bucket of spring water. Now to get to the spring you had to go out a path around the hill, go through a gate and cross a little branch to the spring house, where milk and butter were kept.

A strange thing happened that morning. As I was walking around the hill, I saw an animal about the size of a cat lying in front of me. I had never seen anything like it. It had a rat-like face, coarse grayish-white hair on its body, a pig-like snout, long naked ears and a large hairless scaly tail. Thinking it was dead; I walked around it and went on my way to the spring. When I came back, it was not there.

I told my father about the dead animal I saw in the path and that it wasn't there when I came back, and I knew I had seen it.

My father said, "Child, that was a possum." When they think they are in danger, they lie still and play like they are dead. From this habit, we get the expression 'playing possum'.

Then I began asking questions about the possum. I learned that its real name was opossum and that the Virginia opossums were the best known. When they are born, they are so small that 15-18 will fit in a teaspoon. They are even smaller than honeybees. When their young are born, they find their way into an external pouch on the skin of the abdomen and stay there until they are about 5 weeks old; at which time, they climb to the mother's back and depend on her for several weeks more.

The mother seems to know when they can care for themselves and then shakes them off.

They use their tails to hang from the tree branches. They have very sharp claws and teeth and prowl at night. They eat almost any kind of animal or vegetable. Their flesh is

82

white and sometimes in the South they are baked with sweet potatoes.

That sneaky opossum sure fooled me!

GRANDMOTHER'S QUILT

A story written as though Jennifer Beulah Fox's granddaughter is actually telling the story to her granddaughter.

Our house had become so crowded. Father had promised to remodel the attic, making two extra rooms. I thought at last I can have a room of my own. Mother was busy working at the office every day. Looking at me she said, "I will need some help and you can help me."

The next day I began dragging dusty trunks and boxes out from the eaves of the attic. In one box I found ribbon, post cards, shells, wooden spools and a faded blue book with its title **With Love** in silver letters centered on the front. On the spine of the book were the initials B.S.F. I wondered if the F stood for Fox. I remember Mother telling me that my Grandmother Jennifer's Grandmother Fox had written a book for Grandmother Jennifer. I, too, remember her telling me that Grandmother Jennifer, for whom I was named, had one brother, Nelson, whose middle name was Fox. I opened the book.

One the first page was written: With love to my granddaughter, Jennifer Law, for whom this book was written. Leafing through the book I found that Grandmother Fox loved quilts. I closed the book and laid it aside to read later. Then I opened another box. Packed inside a pillow case was something soft. I pulled it out and found a quilt. Written on a yellowed piece of paper and pinned to the quilt were these words:

> Jennifer Bancroft Law
> 10 years, 7 months , 28 days
> Rt. 3, High Point Ridge Road
> Franklin, Tennessee 37064

Mother had told me that Grandmother Jennifer had saved a quilt for me, which her Grandmother Fox had made her. I think the same grandmother that wrote the book must have made the quilt. Until then I didn't know that grandmothers had grandmothers! Each of the twenty squares seemed to represent something. Squares were joined with red which reminded me of picture frames.

I closed my eyes and tried to picture Grandmother Jennifer when she was a little girl. Was she tall? Did I look like her? Did she have long or short hair? She must have loved me very much to have saved this quilt for me. And her Grandmother Fox must have loved her very much to have made it for her.

Time passed fast. It was getting hot and stuffy. Dozing, a parade of events passed before me. We, my father, mother and I, were living there very long until there were two little Laws, for a new baby came into the family, Nelson Fox Law. He seemed small to have such a big name. His father liked the initials for they also stood for National Football League. Mother brought him home from the hospital and I held him. He began to squirm and give a loud cry as if to say, "Sissy, you are holding me too tight."

I was sick and would have to have an operation. I was born with two holes in between my heart chambers. As time went on my condition became worse. I was taken regularly to the Medical College of Virginia at Richmond for check-ups.

Now I was five years old. My bags were packed for a trip to the hospital. Packed with my clothes were a teddy bear named George and a pillow with a smiley face on it. I had carried the pillow around for days before I left.

When I got to Richmond I found that many sections of the city did not have drinking water. Due to a recent flood the hospital had canceled operations for the next few days. I was lucky. I had a good place to stay where the water was all right. The waters remained high for the next few days washing lumber across the highways.

Then one day my Grandmother Law said, "I have been praying about this and today's going to be the day." She was right. The telephone rang telling my parents to bring me to the hospital.

I dreaded it but was looking forward to the time that I could run, jump and play as other children did.

In preparation for the surgery a nurse brought in a little doll and fastened some tubes to it. She told me when I woke up from the operation I would look like that. I said, "Will I have blond hair?"

Another nurse came in and gave me a shot. Grandmother Fox told me a story she had read when she was a little girl. The story was about an old mother hen that had hatched some eggs. Along with the chickens hatched was a little duck hatched from a duck egg that had got mixed with the other eggs. She told me about how worried the mother hen was as she watched the little duck get into the water. Grandmother placed a pillow under my head. Some men came and wheeled me down the hall. Grandmother and Poppaw went with me as far as the elevator.

The next day after the operation I saw my parents briefly. On the third day a nurse helped me and I walked down the hall. I asked for a doughnut and said, " bring little Mary my friend one. She's not very happy."

The scene changed. I was holding my little baby brother, Nelson, tending him in the back seat of the car. He was crying. The motion of the car did not quiet him. Mother said, "If you won't hold him so tight he will stop crying."

I said, " He is the only little brother I have and I am trying to take care of him."

It was Fall of 1972, I was attending Carrboro School. I was the only little girl with a long scar that reached to my neckline. I wore high necked dresses so it would not show.

Now it is Thanksgiving time. Mother and Daddy had promised to take me to Disney World after my operation. This was the day I have been anticipating for months. We went down in an airplane, my first plane ride.

We are living in Nashville, Tennessee. Fresh on his feet, running and playing, was a gray pony with white spots. I called to him. He whined and whimpered kicked up his hells and came to me. I gave him an ear of corn and named him Indian. Then I rode on him down the hill toward home.

Nelson was riding behind me. My father was walking along beside me. "Giddy up", my father said. Nelson said, "Nop, Daddy, giddy down."

It's getting warmer and warmer. I am at Sunset Beach, I love to walk in the water, collect shells, and sand dollars while watching the tide come in.

I am backstage at the Grand Ole Opry. What fun it is getting autographs of the stars. Oh, I got Grandpa Jones's autograph and my picture made with Roy Acuff.

Next I visit my grandparents at their cabin, 'Foxes Den', on New River. I looked at Papa's garden and said, " It must have taken a lot of little seeds."

The next day we went fishing at Willowton, West Virginia. I did not have any bait. The caretaker gave me some kernels of canned corn. I began catching fish. Just as I pulled out a big one I awoke.

Mother had come in from work. I heard her say, "Jennifer, Jennifer, where are you?" Had I been dreaming? It was so real.

I said, "Mother, I remember who I am. I am glad you named me Jennifer after my grandmother. I went to sleep and did not get all the boxes unpacked. Do you think I could take Grandmother's quilt to school and tell about the things she did when she was a little girl? I know a lot of things I can tell."

Mother said, "Slow down, I don't see why not. I'm glad you found Grandmother's quilt. I will take it down to school for you. After that, you may use it for a wall hanging. We will clean the attic another time."

MY STRAW HAT

I wore blue checked dresses with a belt behind that buttoned on one side. The dress had a peter pan collar and buttoned down the back. It was called an apron but had no resemblance to an apron of today.

I also wore shoes, not slippers, and long black socks. I hated the long black socks because they were so hot.

Mother insisted that I wear a bonnet, but I always carried mine by the strings and dragged the bonnet in the dirt. Mother finally "gave up" on me and bought me a straw hat.

I liked my straw hat !

"Misty"

(A read aloud story for children)
by: Beulah S. Fox
Copyright 1985
Reprinted from Mountain Laurel December 1985

It was Christmas Eve 1977. A large evergreen tree, dressed in gold ornaments, dominated the living room at Granddaddy Law's house in Bishopville, SC. Never had there been as many presents – thin ones, fat ones and a large one. Jennifer fondled each one and tried to guess its contents. Then she started begging her grandparents and Uncle John to open the packages on Christmas Eve. The family finally agreed to let her open one package. She tore into the package and found a small hair drier from her parents. This satisfied her. She'd have to wait.

The next morning finally came. Going to church with her parents helped to take her mind off the presents. Grandma Law stayed at home and prepared the lunch.

After the lunch, Jennifer was told that she could distribute the gifts. She tried to be very fair about it. Giving each person a gift, then starting over again. Each one opened the gift and held it up for the others to see and enjoy before the next person opened his gift. The big box was opened last. It was a king-size puff quilt for Jennifer's mother.

Everybody seemed very happy because of the beautiful gifts received. That is, everybody but Jennifer. She seemed grateful but had a thoughtful look on her face. Then she looked at her mother and said, "I like everything that I got, but I would rather have a little puppy than all of this." Her mother heard and remembered what she said.

On the next Tuesday Jennifer and her family returned home to Nashville. Nothing more was said about the puppy. As soon as Mother could get things unpacked, she took Jennifer downtown to the S.P.C.A.

Just as they arrived, a puppy was being delivered there, a beautiful white puppy that appeared to be part Dachshund and part Terrier. Jennifer immediately fell in love with her and wanted her for her own. Mother bought the puppy for her. As they were going home, Mother said, "What are you going to name her?" "It's beginning to rain. I shall call her Misty" said Jennifer.

They stopped by the library and got a book on how to train pets.. Jennifer began training the dog. Before long, Misty would whine when she wanted out, shake hands with you and roll over. She seemed to love her new owner.

Jennifer said, "Mother, you know what? This is the best Christmas I've ever had. This is Misty's best Christmas too." Misty barked as if to say, "That's right!"

Papa's Jelly

Spring came early that year, Yellow forsythias began blooming. And the birds began feeding their young. Grandmother and Papa began getting "cabin fever". They knew that the water could be turned on in the cabin and it was time for the garden to be planted.

So they packed their clothes and food in the back of the little truck and headed for the cabin. All the way up Commissary Hill and around the mountain the cabin called. Grandmother thought I can't wait until I get there as she enjoyed the patterns the shade made on the dirt road.

When they arrived they unpacked and enjoyed the peace and quiet of the river. Everything went well until Papa said,

" Oh, I forget my jelly."

Now Papa loved grape jelly. He ate it for breakfast with toast, and for lunch and supper for dessert. Grandmother knew Papa wasn't going to be too happy without his jelly. So she said, "Let me drive out and get you some jelly."

"No," he said, " I'll do without it this time." Papa was never one to cause others inconvenience.

About that time a knock came at the door. When Papa answered the door there stood a young woman, Mrs. L., who had lived near the cabin for several months but had never visited us before. In her hand was a paper bag.

She said, "I brought you a mess of young apples."

Papa said, "Thanks." He brought the bag into the kitchen and was emptying the apples. Guess what? In the bottom of that bag was a pint jar of grape jelly.

God has a way of making himself felt in our lives.

Did He put it into Mrs. L's heart to bring the apples and jelly?

Did she want the jelly to be a surprise? I believe that God work in mysterious ways.

Can you think of any other reason?

EARLY SCHOOL YEARS

I don't know what kept boys and girls from getting hurt when I was a little girl in school. At recess time the boys and girls went wild. We knew exactly how far we could play Follow the Leader, jumping the branch up the hollow, turning and jumping down the branch, getting back to school just in time for the bell.

Then we'd line up in front of the door and walk in as quietly as little angels.

Another thing we did was to play Follow the Leader through an old empty house. It was ready to fall in with nails sticking up on the floor boards throughout the house. The house had been plastered using strips of wood to hold the plaster. Holes through the walls provided places for the leader to run through and the others to follow.

On the outside of the old house was an old well covered with rotten boards. We peeped through the boards to see what we could see.

In Winter time when snow was on the ground we climbed a steep hill behind the school and used wash tubs for sleighs.

I don't recommend any of this. "It's better to be safe than sorry."

My sister, brother and I had gone up to the edge of the mountain to bring the turkeys home.

I was running barefooted when I jumped over a coiled rattlesnake. The three of us threw rocks until we killed the snake. Then because the snake had a strange looking tail I put it across a stick and carried it to a neighbor's house saying. "Look what a strange looking snake we have killed."

The neighbor said, "Child, you have killed a rattlesnake with seven rattlers on it."

The Little Boy Who Asked Questions

(A story for Nelson)
by: Beulah S. Fox
copyright 1985
Reprinted from Mountain Laurel, August 1985

"Grandmuver, where's my quilt?" asked the five-year-old boy.

Grandmother didn't know what to say. She had made his big sister an Album Quilt showing events in her life, thinking someday when the little boy was older, she'd make him a quilt.

The little boy thought Grandmother could do anything, but he didn't think this was fair.

Later Grandmother said to Pop-paw, "I feel bad about not having a quilt for him. I had planned to make him one when he got older." Pop-paw said, "I don't know, he's done many of the same things that Jennifer has. It would be interesting for him to know who his ancestors were. He's ridden an airplane too. Remember how he likes all kinds of animals and how he enjoys special holidays and stories. I loved the way he wanted a calculator when he was in kindergarten.

And how he said the had always wanted to sleep in a big bed and wanted a fishing pole for his birthday so he could go fishing with Pop-paw at the cabin.

It's sweet how he always says, "I'm fine" when you talk to him on the phone.

Do you recall the time when we were riding along in the red GMC truck and he said, "Pop-paw what's B-U-M-P spell?" About that time the truck went over it. He said "Never mind!"

What was the little bear's name he took to bed with

him? "Tut-tut." "Yes, that's it."

"Oh, yes, the weeping willow trees that he called crying trees and the half-river. Remember the time we were crossing New River on the Narrows bridge when he looked at Wolf Creek going into New River and said, "Look Pop-paw, a half-river."

And the time we took him to the Grand Ole Opry and how he had to stay indoors so much last winter during the snow.

Grandmother said, "You have given me some good ideas." She set to work. She used blue flannel to make the sky and yellow-green embroidery thread to make the Grand Ole Opry and on another, a big snowman. Near the bottom of the quilt she embroidered these works: Made in 1977, so the little boy would remember the year in which the quilt was made.

People saw Grandmother working on the quilt and said, "I'd like to know why you are spending so much time on the quilt. It would be so much easier to buy a blanket." Grandmother had never been used to having things easy, so she paid no attention and kept on working. As she worked, she thought about the good times she would have when the little boy came to spend his vacation with her.

Grandmother told Pop-paw, "When I quilt it, I will sew around the trees, the butterflies, and the bear so he can enjoy the pictures." She joined the quilt with blue like the little boy's blue jeans.

The people said, "You have so many things to do, why don't you get someone to quilt it?" Grandmother said, " I want to make every little stitch so that he can look at it with pride and say, "My Grandmother made it". And she kept on working. While she worked, she kept asking herself, "Will he like it? What will he say?"

After five days of straight quilting, using two hundred fifty (250) yards of thread and millions of little stitches, the quilt was finished. When Grandmother had finished quilting it she spread it out on the bed, People came and looked at it. They said, "We have never seen anything like it."

The little boy came to spend his vacation with his grandparents. Grandmother kept watching the little boy to see when he would notice the quilt. His eyes got big and he said, "Grandmuver, is zat my quilt?" Then he gave Grandmother a big bear hug. One look at the little boy's face and Grandmother knew why she had spent days making the quilt. "After all," she said, "He's the only little grandson I have."

After the little boy saw the quilt, Grandmother read this story to him. She said, " Who do you think the little boy was?" And the little boy asked another question, "Was it Nelson?"

"PASS IT ON"

It was about like any, other morning. At exactly 7:00 I picked up my school bag and headed for school.

As I went out the door each morning I looked up at Angel's Rest and repeated the first two verses of the 121st Psalm: "I will lift up mine eyes unto the hills. From whence cometh my help? My help cometh from the Lord who made heaven and earth." This got me off to a good day. Then I would go on my way.

Half way to school that morning I realized I had a flat tire. I pulled over enough to get off the road and stopped. Thinking I knew how to change the tire, I took the spare out of the back and rolled it around to the side of the car. Just then a car stopped and a young man got out. He said, "Lady, I'll change that tire for you."

In a few minute the man had the tire changed. I was so grateful. Taking out my check book I said, "To whom do I make this check out?"

"Lady, you don't owe me anything. I had car trouble at Rich Creek this morning and some man helped me get started. He told me to pass it on. Just pass it on to someone else".

"The man never told me his name. Since that time I have tried to "pass it on" .

AN EARLY MORNING ADVENTURE

By: Beulah S. Fox
Copyright 1987
Reprinted from Mountain Laurel, June 1987

I know where you can find some big blackberries, my dad said. "If you and Ruth would be careful crossing the fences – there were two of them– you could take your buckets and pick enough berries for Mother to bake a pie." That sounded like fun to us. He told us to go across the bridge, cross the fence, go down by the creek until we came to a second wire fence and cross it.

Just on the other side by the creek there was some bottom land with a hill behind it. In the bottom by the creek we would find some wild blackberries. He said they grew best there because the loam was deep, mellow and damp and that there were plenty of young vines which had grown from the roots of the old plants.

We dressed as though it was winter wearing Dad's long sleeved shirts, and our brother's overalls with high top shoes and bonnets tied under our chins. Mother had told me to be sure to keep my bonnet on, for I had a history of taking it off and dragging it on the ground.

After we crossed the bridge, we were careful to help each other over the fences. Finally, carrying our lard buckets, we came to the tangles and thicket of blackberries. There we saw berries that looked to us like swollen jewels. We put one in our bucket and two in our mouths. The berries were on growths that looked like little thimbles which stayed on the stem when the fruit was picked. We were careful not to pick the red ones or the ones that were too soft. The berries were so big that it didn't take long to fill our five-pint buckets.

Just as our buckets were about full we noticed a little animal that we thought was a pretty little kitten playing around near us. It was the size of small kitten, had a long pointed nose, arched back and short legs. It's fur was long, thick, and shiny black with a white stripe down the back. It had a white patch on its forehead, tail long and bushy, black on top with white underneath, very attractive. It walked like a person that had on shoes that were too tight.

We decided we wanted it for a pet and began chasing it. It ran through a patch of skunk cabbage, a soft-stemmed plant which is found in low swamps, and then started up the hill. We ran behind it. There were times we almost had it, but the beautiful creature got away.

We took our berries home and gave them to Mother for a pie. When we told her about the little pet getting away, Mother replied, "That was no kitten; it was a skunk." We had frightened the little skunk and he had squirted out fluid with considerable force. Even after Mother washed our clothes and we bathed in the creek, the powerful unpleasant odor stayed around for awhile.

THE UGLY VALENTINE

By: Beulah S. Fox

Copyright 1986

Reprinted from Mountain Laurel , February 1986

There are several different explanations for the custom of sending valentines on Valentine's Day. All of them are probably inaccurate. The most plausible is that Valentine's Day is a survival of a February 5th Roman Festival. It was once the custom to draw lots to decide which young man and woman should be each other's valentine for the coming year. The couples would then exchange gifts, and sometimes they even became engaged.

In the '30s some valentines were printed on a sheet of cheap paper and might read something like this, a picture of an old maid at the top of the paper and a verse saying:

You're afraid of your shadow and
scared of a mouse.
Wouldn't you feel safer
With a man in the house?

You would have to have known my Grandmother to fully appreciate this valentine story. Grandmother was probably 80 years old. No one knew when she was born. Once I searched the court house records. In it I found her birthday recorded, turned a few pages and there it was recorded differently, one birthday in August and one in November.

Anyway Grandma liked to wear red, had gray hair that wandered out of place, doing what it wanted to do, just like Grandma herself. She said exactly what she thought, sometimes hurting peoples feelings. To me that was a part of her and I loved her very much.

Holidays meant little to her. It was special if she ate

100

with us on a holiday. But one day all of that changed. I never remembered Grandma getting a piece of mail. My Grandpa got some mail. Grandma couldn't read or write. She learned to count by counting eggs. On this day an envelope came addressed to her: Mrs. Christena Stowers, Cove Creek, Va. She recognized her name and got very excited. She opened it and there was an ugly valentine. This was in the '30s.

An old woman in a red dress and apron was sitting in a chair with a huge mouth. Below the picture was a verse about gossiping. Now I knew my grandmother didn't gossip. She didn't talk a lot. She just said what she thought. I was thinking, "Who did this? Why did they want to hurt a sweet old lady?"

About that time I noticed Grandmother. She wasn't acting as I thought she'd be. She was so happy, very happy. Somebody had sent her some mail.

She was proud of that valentine, so proud that she tacked it up above the table and left it there. When she had company, which was often, she would point to the valentine. Until her death that valentine was the only picture hanging in her dining room.

WHY JERRY NEVER GETS COLD

School had just begun. It was hot, dusty and dry. Seven year old Jerry came running in from school, up the steps, and straight to the refrigerator.

Her father had taken a Coke bottle and put some anti-freeze in it and put it in the freezer to see if it would freeze. He was trying to see how much Anti-freeze he needed for his car. Another gallon that had been opened sat on the landing at the top of the steps.

Jerry lifted the Coke bottle thinking it was soda and drank it. Then she said, "Mother, what was in that bottle in the refrigerator?" Mother said, "Oh no, I hope you didn't drink it! That was anti-freeze." Mother kept telling herself, "Don't panic, think."

The only thing Mother could think of to kill poison was milk. She gave her a glass of milk to drink.

Then she went outside the room to check the can of anti-freeze at the top of the steps. The first thing she noticed was the symbol of the skull which meant it was very poisonous.

She ran back, grabbed the quart bottle of milk and began making Jerry drink the milk. After she drank a glass and caught her breath, Mother would make her drink more until she had drunk a quart. Then Mother let her stop.

Now we are going for a walk. They walked up to Uncle Wade's. There were no cars around to transport her to doctor or hospital. Everyone except the older people who could not drive was away at work. Jerry's father was working 3-11 shift at the Celanese plant.

Jerry never became sick. So we believed that she had tasted the anti-freeze and spit it out. It never bothered her in any way.

However, it helped her in one way. All the way through

elementary and high school she wrote about her experience. Each year she would write an essay telling why she never got cold. It was an unusual experience and she usually received an "A" on her paper.

BACKYARD BEAUTY

By: Beulah S. Fox
Copyright 1986
Reprinted from Blue Ridge Digest

When we moved to a log cabin on Wolf Creek in Giles County, with the Creek running at the edge of our backyard, we never expected to inherit some wild ducks. It started with a mother duck setting on eleven eggs in a warm nest made from leaves, dry grass and other materials, lined with down from the mother's own breast. It was built on the ground near the water. We later found that some ducks set on as many as sixteen eggs. We checked on her every few days. Then one day her nest was empty except for the egg shells. We knew she had hatched. It took approximately four weeks to hatch. We looked up and down the creek and spotted her swimming close to the bank with seven little ducklings. Mother duck had led them to the creek as soon as they were able to travel.

We learned that they swim before they eat and may not eat until the next day, except for insects from the creek. Mother guarded them carefully. She would dive at you if you attempted to pick up one. They were about six weeks old when they began to fly. Meanwhile they lived together in a flock. Guess who fed them? At first Elmer, my husband, bought corn for them. They also ate insects, snails, grain, grasses and other kinds of plant life. Later we learned they would eat almost anything except onions.

The male mallards are beautifully colored during the breeding season and in winter, are grayish brown on back and purple underneath. Their heads are a glossy blue-green that is iridescent. The lower back, rump, and tail covers are glossy black. The tails are white with two white and two black bars on each of the side wings. White bands circle the necks. The bills are olive green and feet are orange-red.

The female mallards are not as brilliantly colored as the males.

Just before a storm, they will leave and in a few days, be back begging for food. When the creek is frozen over, it's hard for them to find food, so we feed them a little extra.

We have learned several things about them. When the leader stretches her neck up and down, the others follow sometimes in a straight row. They seem to know when a storm is approaching. When they are flying high, they like to land in water. One time, during the winter, when the creek was frozen over, they kept circling our house like an airplane getting ready for a landing. We knew they were up there, but they didn't come down until they could land in water. They hadn't forgotten where their food was.

They experience danger in order to hatch and raise their family. One duck built her nest in a brushy field farther back from the water, joining the state highway. The highway men cut the weeds growing over her nest with a long sickle. She came back and set in the hot sun until her eggs hatched. This mother duck thought she really had this nest hidden. She would come to the house to eat, take a bath in the creek and them go back to her nest. Instead of going straight to her next, she went at a right angle, looking back all the time to see if anyone had spotted her. She came to eat at the same time every day. I thought she must be setting. One day I followed her and learned her secret she thought was so well kept.

One duck set on a bank in front of the house. The bank was overgrown with brambles and weeds. It was Spring and Elmer and I decided to burn off the bank and plant some vetch as a ground cover. We burned off the bank not knowing that a duck was setting there. The fire burned up to the nest and jumped over the nest without disturbing a single egg. Smoke caused the duck to fly off. We were worried that she wouldn't go back to the nest. She did. Then one day she proudly brought seven little ducklings around the to back porch to show us her babies. We tried to feed them, but they wouldn't eat. She took them for a swim, spent the night away and came back to eat the next day.

This story began three years ago. Various numbers of ducks come and go. We have had as many as 32 ducks. Today I counted 20. They know their corn comes from the garage. If they see you on the back porch or in the back door, they will come out of the creek and beat you to the garage. Only one is named. We call him Foreigner. He flew in one day and never left. The white band around his neck is wider, thus we can recognize him from the others. At first the others did not accept him. Now he's one of them.

At first the ducks liked Elmer best. They would always come out of the creek when he was around. Then I noticed if I wore his overall jacket, they'd come out for me. Now they are friendly to both of us. If we sleep late in the morning, they'll come to our bedroom window begging. I think we started something. But if you get to really know them, you couldn't help but like them. Guess who I hear at my back door?

An Unexpected Visitor...

It had been a long wintry day. The snow had covered the ground and was still falling. As I was driving home, I planned what I was going to do when I arrived. Elmer was working 3-11. I thought how good a pot of vegetable soup would taste. So I began making soup. When I had put everything together I had about 6 quarts. Then I decided to make an apple pie.

Dark came and with it came a knock at the door. I opened it and there facing me was a strange woman. She said, "I am Jimmy's aunt. I came to see him but he is not at home." Jimmy was the boy next door who had recently lost his parents.

I said, "Come in and stay with me tonight". She came in. The soup was still hot on the stove and the apple pie hot from the oven. I didn't have to think what I could fix her for supper. I filled a large soup bowl full of soup and cut a piece of apple pie. Then I poured a glass of milk.

You made the soup after you came home from school, she said. "Why did you make so much?" "I don't know," I said. "I really don't."

"I'm glad you did. It is delicious!"

APPLE BUTTER

APPLE BUTTER is a spread for bread made by cooking apples to a thick consistency and seasoning with spices usually oil of cinnamon. When I was growing up, making APPLE BUTTER was a fall rite and actually a two-day affair. There are eight gallons of apples to every bushel.

We used two bushels of Ben Davis apples. Any cooking apple will do. The first day we peeled, cored, and sliced one bushel of apples and made applesauce. This gave us a head start.

On the morning of the APPLE BUTTER making the copper kettle was scoured and cleaned with vinegar and salt. After building a fire to a medium heat beneath the kettle, we put the pre-cooked apples in with enough water to cover the bottom of the kettle.

In the meantime we pre-cooked the second bushel the same as the first apple sauce consistency and continued to add the applesauce until the two bushels were in the kettle cooking, stirring constantly to ensure even cooking and no burned spots, resulting in sore muscles the next day.

Half way through cooking we added two pounds of sugar to every gallon of apples constantly stirring the APPLE BUTTER for about seven hours, depending upon desired thickness. The longer we cooked the redder and better it got. One hour before cooking was completed, we added cinnamon to taste and canned in quart cans to preserve. We spread it freshly on a butter biscuit or an old-time fruitcake, spreading apple butter between the layers.

My Grandmother Walters used to make these fruitcakes at Christmas. How we grandchildren liked them! She used a

Stack Cake

1-1/2 cup shortening
2 cups sugar
2 eggs
1/2 cup molasses
4 cups flour
2 teaspoons soda
2 teaspoons cloves
2 teaspoons cinnamon
2 teaspoons ginger

Cream shortening and sugar. Beat in eggs. Add molasses and sifted dry ingredients. Pat dough out in shallow pans and bake in moderate oven until done. When layers are cooled, spread with APPLE BUTTER and stack. Makes six thin layers.

Yum, Yum!

A Rural School Teacher

My own experience seemed more rural than that in our program book, so I have chosen it instead. As far back as I can remember, I wanted to become a teacher. I used to gather my playmates around me in a coal house, coal in one end, school in the other end.

I worked my way through college, waiting tables, ironing shirts and being janitor. The janitor work proved to be valuable training for written in my first contract were these words. "School room to be kept clean by the teacher." Farther down on the page was written Board reserves right to shorten term in case funds become exhausted.

New teachers were sent to one of two places. If you could teach this year out, it meant you would be moved to a more convenient place the following year.

I had 45 pupils and 7 grades. I did everything that first year but play football with them. Many times we had to circle the pot-bellied stove in order to keep warm. The school board – this was in another county – would pay for just so many cords of wood. If you used all the wood, you did without or some kind patron donated some.

There were no hot lunches. On Friday, we would boil a potato or make hot chocolate to supplement our bag lunches. This was a real treat.

Today I teach in a modern building with electric heat, cafeteria, primary teacher, teacher's aide, cook and janitor. It's impossible for me to enter the building without being grateful for a warm building with plenty of supplies.

I have found children to be delightful and very unpredictable. A few years ago one of my fifth grade boys was reading for opening exercises the 60th Psalm from the

King James version that says, "O God thou has cast us off". He said instead, "O God Thou has cussed us out".

Last year one little pre-schooler was visiting our school. Just before he went home, he asked if he might say something. His teacher told him he could. He marched to the front of the room and said, "You know what I think? I think I'm going to like school".

This past week I was trying to get the idea across of the importance of being accurate in measuring and counting. I asked the class to think of an example at school where counting incorrectly would make a difference. One little girl said, "Suppose we sent in the lunch count as 50 (we usually have about 30). Then I asked what difference that would make. I expected the answer to be a waste of food and money. The little boy answered, "We'd all get seconds". The rewards are many!

As a teacher I know that I am dealing with a changing situation. The child is an ever-challenging individual who grows and develops with each new experience. I am glad to have part in his growth. I know that I must determine his potential and then get him to work to that capacity. In order to do this, I must both encourage and challenge him. I must teach him it is far more honorable to fail than to cheat and teach him also to have faith in his own ideas.

I have reached out to my pupils. The greater the need and hunger, the more compassion I have felt for the child.

More is being expected of today's teachers than ever before. The challenge is great.

I like the philosophy in our program book that says: To lead the ideal life, one must accept its hard spots and its soft, its heavens and its hells. It should be enjoyed for its todays, with sure knowledge that, with God's help, if each day is made as good as it can be, surely the unknown tomorrow's which are entirely in His hand will be all right.

111

My Three Most Memorable Teachers

I have had many good teachers but probably the three who meant the most to me were my first grade teacher, Ada Walters (Mother's sister), my eighth grade teacher, Trula Stowers, and Dr. Homer Howard, my advisor in graduate school.

The first one I remember fondly, Miss Ada. She boarded at our home. I walked with her two miles a day. I was five years old at the time. She was teaching in a one-room school and had gotten permission for me to attend, since I wasn't old enough. I remember walking and trying very hard to take big steps so I could keep up with her. She loved children and they knew it.

Miss Trula was my eighth grade teacher. She taught three of us after she had taught all seven grades all day in a one-room school. She charged us two dollars a month, yes a month. She carried books to us, for we had no library. She made learning come alive. I can remember her teaching us Scott's Lady of the Lake. I can still see some of the scenes in that book. They were so real. On my report card, she wrote: "I love you, oh so much". I loved her too. She was probably the most dedicated teacher I have every known.

When I entered graduate school, I had heard that Dr. Howard was an excellent advisor, if you could get him. I asked him to be my advisor. He was overloaded with work and declined.

I was assigned to another young professor who helped me get started on my work. Then he ran away with one of his students.

I was talking to Dr. Howard about it. He said, "I'll help you." My work was lost and I had to start over. Dr. Howard was very precise. I wrote and rewrote. Finally, he graded the thesis and I was given an A on it. Not only was he kind, he was willing to go the second mile or beyond the call of duty.

Nelson and Patrick Get Baptized

On Sunday, June 1, a crowd of people gathered on a raised spot surrounded by a rock wall under a giant sycamore tree on the bank of Wolf Creek at Boom Park for baptizing. The creek was about the width of the river Jordan where John baptized many Christians. This ceremony is a ceremony of washing done to one who accepts the Christian faith and has been used since the day of Jesus Christ when he told his disciples to go and teach all nations baptizing them in the name of the Father and the Son and the Holy Spirit.

It was a beautiful day with a hint of a cool breeze. The water was flowing gently and peace like a dove hovered over the place. Soon there came two youths dressed in white robes for baptism. The minister, a young man himself, called the boys apart from the others and gave them some instructions, then turned to the congregation and read some scripture. Then, without hesitation, he walked into the water. He was followed by Nelson, the older boy, who was baptized first. After which, Patrick followed.

As I watched I thought of another baptism that took place sixty plus years ago. This is how it happened.

When I was a little girl, heavy farm wagons carried products to market and people to where ever they needed to go. My father had one of these but he also had what he called a spring wagon. This wagon was smaller and was equipped with springs for easier riding. When the family had to go somewhere, he took the spring wagon. We did not have a car until many years later.

My family had heard about a baptism about three miles down the road on a Sunday afternoon. We put on our Sunday-best clothes and started out, the children in the back of the wagon and Mother and Daddy seated on the wagon seat with Daddy driving. Daddy had put some hay in the wagon bed to make it ride even better.

When we arrived at the spot where the baptism was to take place a crowd of people had gathered on the bank of the creek talking quietly and waiting. The minister led the crowd in singing a song entitled, "Jesus Loves Even Me". I listened but it didn't make any sense to me. My father, a Sunday school superintendent for many years and my mother had taught me that Jesus loves me. But when my friend Eva and her mother were baptized I thought the song was saying, Jesus loves Eva and me, meaning Eva and her mother. I was hurt and couldn't understand why he didn't love me too. I asked my parents about it and they told me what the song was really saying. Since that time, I know that He loves me too.

As I walked away from the sacred spot, I picked a four-leaf clover and handed it to Nelson. It had been a good day. 1-4-86

THE DAY OF THE EASTER EGG HUNT

It was the last of March with the chill till in the air. Stowersville School, named for the ancestors of some of the pupils who attended, stood just off the dirt road in Bland County, Virginia, showing its age of over a hundred years. Once it had been a larger school, but now it was lucky to have 20 pupils in seven grades and one teacher. The pupils were bright-eyed children of farmers who tilled the surrounding fields.

Teachers had done their best to make the schoolroom livable by whitewashing the walls. Wainscoting came up about a yard from the floor. Many holes had been cut in the wood by pocketknives; the holes were stuffed with paper and broken pencils. A few windows were broken with cardboard tacked in. The sun came in through the high windows spotting the heads of the children and making a pattern on their desks.

On that particular day, excess energies had accumulated, for everyone was looking forward to the Easter egg hunt to be held at 3:00. School was out at 4:00. We had an hour for the party. I felt shy and left out. I felt different because I had long hair. All of the other girls had short hair.

Time came for lunch. We marched out and took our lard buckets which contained our lunch from the shelf in the cloakroom. The girls went to their favorite eating place underneath a large walnut tree in the back of the school. There we sat down and began eating our lunch. Our lunch consisted of meat and apple butter on biscuits. We hurried and played house under the tree. House consisted of a floor plan bounded by rocks.

After playing for a while, we went back to the school building and pulled out some tin, leftover from covering the roof, from under the floor of the building and used it to play jack rocks on. Out jack rocks were small round rocks and treasured for their uniformity. The bell rang and we went back inside. It seemed that 3:00 would never come.

After that, we marched up to the recitation bench to recite our History and Geography. Finally we were allowed to go outside for the Easter egg hunt. That morning each pupil had brought colored eggs dyed with onion hulls and catnip plant. The eggs were hidden by one of the parents while we were in the schoolroom. We were told to look within a certain boundary. It wasn't long until all the eggs were found. A little boy had found the most eggs and received a small prize.

Then our teacher took us about half way up the hill behind the school. She told us we were going to have an egg roll. The object was to roll the egg down the hill about 20 feet into a small hole. Boys and girls tried, each person missing until my turn. I tried and the egg went into the hole. The teacher said, "Beulah, how did you manage to do that?"

I said, "I noticed that everyone was aiming at the hole and missing it about four inches. I tried aiming four inches to the right of where they had started and hoped it would hit the hole. It did. That's all I did." My teacher laughed.

Suddenly I didn't feel so shy anymore. I had done something the others hadn't done. The prize was a box of candy. I couldn't have been happier.

The Day Grandma Got Her New Washer

Grandma's mind was made up. She was going to buy a washing machine. Since she could remember she had gathered the dirty clothes, carried them across the road down under the hill to the creek, filled the iron pot with water and heated it over a hot fire.

She dropped lye soap into the pot so it would melt and make suds. After the water was hot, she scrubbed the white clothes on the washboard first and then she did the colored ones. She washed on the creek bank in the shade of the willow trees so she didn't have to carry water up the hill. Then my grandmother and I carried the wet clothes up the hill and I helped her hang the clothes on the line.

One day she confided to me that she had been saving her butter-and-egg money for a washing machine.

"Grat's getting tired of helping me," she said. "He says it's women's work". Last week I caught him burning some of his socks in the fire to keep from washing them."

She asked me to not tell anybody in the family about her plan. "They would expect me to get my arm caught in the wringer right off the bat," she said, "I think I can manage the machine. I'm awful tired of washing on the board."

I hoped Grandma wouldn't change her mind. I wanted her to have anything in the world that would make her a life a little easier.

Later that same week, Grandma and I were sitting on the front porch resting when we saw a salesman coming down the dusty road in his Model T truck.

He came in and told Grandma about the Maytag gasoline

washing machine and how it operated. Grandma had no water ready so he didn't demonstrate his product. But he did explain in detail how it worked.

He told Grandma to fill the tank with gasoline, add a small cup of oil and then turn the needle as far right as it will go. After that she was to crank it with her foot and then turn the needle to a vertical position after it started.

Grandma was most concerned about the danger of getting her arm caught in the wringer and she expressed her worry to the salesman.

The salesman replied that all she had to do was to turn the handle to the off position. Something told me I had better remember this.

Grandma went straight to the corner cupboard and brought out a syrup can with money in it. She paid the salesman from the can and had money left over. She made me promise not to tell anybody how she happened to get the Maytag. She said, "Now God I say." She was always very serious when she said that.

Grandma wanted to try the machine out the instant the salesman left. I helped her carry the water and heat it. We carefully went over the directions the salesman had given us. Then Grandma turned the pointed needle hit the pedal a few times with her foot and the machine started. The lye soap began to smell. Grandma pushed a gearshift knob on the side of the tub and the washing stopped. It was time to put the clothes through the wringer.

Everything went fine for a while. Then the worst – well, almost the worst – happened. Grandma's sweater got caught in the wringer. There could have been a panic but luckily I was watching and remembered to turn the handle as the salesman had said.

"A body is going to have to be more careful," Grandma said as calmly as she could. "I don't know how I could manage without you. Let's keep what happened a secret. It's nobody's business what we do."

I agreed. I knew she was afraid somebody would laugh

at her if they knew.

Years passed. Grandma quickly got the hang of it and used her gray Maytag as long as she lived. She kept a cover over it and from time to time she proudly showed it to friends and neighbors. It was probably her proudest possession.

One day Grandpa – the skeptical one – laid his hand on my shoulder and said, "Beulah, Christena was right in getting that washing machine, even at her age. It's a known fact that times are changing."

Bandanna in a Peach Tree

By: Beulah S. Fox
copyright 1986
Reprinted from Mountain Laurel, July 1986

Today I wandered back in thought to the scents and sounds of the year 1939. I was a young teacher in a one-room school, Stowersville, Bland County, Virginia. The road that led to the county school was a small dirt road and long. Pupils walked along the dusty road, wading snow in the winter, carrying their book bags and swinging their dinner bucket, usually a lard bucket. They had done their chores early so as not to be late. In pleasant weather they enjoyed the pleasant gentle breezes and the sunbeams played on their faces.

About a hop and jump away, above the schoolhouse, lived an old lady, a farmer's wife. She had remarried and had come to live in this little community. No doubt she was lonely at times. I can see her now as she stood in front of her little cottage, arthritic hands behind her, a starched cotton dress covered by an apron that went over her shoulder, a smile on her round pleasant face and soft, fluffy white hair wound in a bun pinned high on the back of her head. Her husband, a cozy farmer, was as thin as she was plump. He always wore suspenders. The thing I remember most about him was that he was a good handyman and very kind and supportive to his second wife. He had a small garden out back of the house which he tended. Once I made their picture with the garden as a background.

They lived in a small white country house with windows

121

of four panes, a porch with two steps across the front of the house where neighbors shared their day, slanted bench with back and room enough for two, plus some cane-bottomed chairs. In the summertime, a ladder-like trellis at the edge of the porch supported blue morning glories. A peach tree grew by the walk. Clumps of hollyhocks showing off their ruffled dresses grew on each side of the front steps, surrounded by a wire fence with white-washed posts.

A cellar or dairy was built in the foot of the hill behind the little house. This was used as a refrigerator to keep food cool. I have drunk many glasses of buttermilk that came from the dairy.

The little house had simple furnishings with a kind-of-lived-in look, rag rugs on the floor, cushions on the chairs, a lacy scarf on the bureau and crisp white curtains at the windows. Grandma King swept, dusted, washed and loved each humble room, of which there were four: living room, two bedrooms, and kitchen with front and back porch.

She was my third grandmother, who was not my grandmother, but my friend. I called her grandmother and she treated me as a grandchild. One day she sent me word by one of her grandchildren to come up after school was out in the afternoon. She wanted me to answer some mail. Her hands were arthritic and it was painful for her to write. I answered her mail and got it ready to be sent out the next day. Then she told me of a plan she had. "When you see a bandanna in the peach tree, come up and answer my mail and spend the night with me."

In the evenings I would stand on the schoolhouse steps and look up the road to her yard to see if the red bandanna was flying in the wind. It wasn't long until I realized that she was planning it so I could spend all the nights when the weather was bad with her. She could foretell the rain and soft-fallen snow.

I had only a short way to go before I was at home with the door open wide. "Good evening," she would say cheerily,. Then she would tell me to rest a spell while she went to the dairy for a glass of cold buttermilk.

After I rested a bit I would get to work answering her mail, mostly letters to her family. Then she'd fix us some supper. She was always cooking something nice. The pickles and jam were delicious. My heart and hands were calm as I felt the touch of her gentle hands, set the red apples in a wooden bowl on the table and listened to the tea kettle singing gaily on the old wood stove where the wood smoke smelled so fresh. There was a homemade rag rug in front of the old rocking chair I sat in. I learned to love the sunny rooms, the kitchen clean and bright and the shelter for the night.

Sun had dropped and I had a home and daily bread and love. Comforting thought prevailed as I lay against a sheet, snowy white. The golden light of the coming day awoke me to the sound of a fire being built, followed by the smell of sausage frying, homemade bread with butter and apple jelly. It was time to go back to the schoolhouse and to watch for the red bandanna in the peach tree.

THRESHING

By: Beulah S. Fox
Copyright 1986
Reprinted from Mountain Laurel July, 1986

When summer had ended and the wheat fields were waving with ripe golden grain, along came the old-fashioned threshing machine. This large steel machine was one of the most important pieces of farm equipment. Not every farmer had a threshing machine. There were only two in the valley where I grew up.

The farmers gathered with suntanned faces covered with chaff to work with the threshing machine, in a community, until all the wheat was threshed, about 12 to 15 men, plus an extra one or two who tagged along for the meal. Then that crew rested and another crew took over.

Farmers used the machine at harvest time to separate wheat from the stalks and hulls. It was driven by a tractor motor connected to it by a belt. The bundles of grain were thrown onto a huge belt and carried into the threshing part of the machine. Through a carriage or pipe, the straw traveled on the belt to a stacker. Here it was blown out to the stack or rick nearby. There might be a long train of teams coming in from the fields, four men on the stack, one throwing bundles to the man doing the feeding, one cutting bands and two measuring grain. Finally the clean golden grain went into sacks and two or three men hauled it into the granary.

We children stood at a distance and watched with awe and carried zinc buckets of spring water for the big threshing crew.

While all of this was happening, down at the house the womenfolk were busy as could be. The day before word had come, "The threshers will be at your house for dinner". There was probably never a housewife but what dreaded to hear those words. First she went to the spring house for plenty of water, milk and butter.

Pies were made the day before and placed in the spring house. My father's favorite pie was custard. My grandfather's favorite pie was raspberry with butter and honey on top. So at our house, we made custard and raspberry pies.

I still remember the custard pie recipe:

1 pint of rich milk
2 eggs
3 tablespoons sugar
1 teaspoon lemon flavoring

All were mixed together and poured into a half-baked crust and baked in a hot oven.

My father always had to have lemon flavoring. Then came piles of potatoes. Mother usually quartered and baked them in a shallow pan with strips of country bacon on top. Then there were greens, green beans, tomatoes, apples, hot biscuits and country butter with milk and coffee basin of water, soap and towel were placed on the porch where the hungry crew washed and marched into the kitchen.

Eight people could eat at a time around the long oil cloth covered table with chairs around three sides and a bench at the back side. There would be two tables of threshers. How they ate, and ate, and ate, until the table was bare except for the pears and apples on the tablecloth! All the time they were seeing who could tell the biggest tales. One that I remember was telling about the day when the machine broke down. One of the men took the piece to be fixed.

Meanwhile, dinner time came around. The men began talking abo,ut going to eat. One of the boys who lived there said, "No work, no eat." It didn't matter where they started, how much they were delayed by rain, they seemed to manage to eat at the same places every year. Word got around where the food was best.

They might finish by middle evening and move the machine to its next place so as to be ready to begin again next morning. But first they would send a messenger to the next place saying, "Threshers will be at your place tomorrow for dinner."

Modern day combines can do more in a short span of time than a dozen men could do in a day with the threshing machine. But somehow I miss the neighborly scene of neighbor helping neighbor using the old fashioned threshing machine.

BEGINNING

TEACHER✓

By: Beulah S. Fox
Copyright 1985
Reprinted from Mountain Laurel September 1985

I was nineteen at the time, a brand new teacher assigned to a one-room school that I had never seen. The road that led to the country school was a narrow dirt road and long. Upon the brow of a little hill the building stood. It was there that I enrolled forty-five pupils, grades 1-7.

I had room and board with a good family who charged me ten dollars a month. My salary was sixty-five dollars a month. I usually went home on the weekends.

I walked two miles a day and carried my books and biscuits. School opened at 9:00 and closed at 4:00. I stayed another half hour to sweep the floor. In order to do this I had to move desks, sweep, then move the desks back in place. The pupils gathered pine knots and built the fires and carried the water from the well. There were two toilets out back, one for the boys and one for the girls. I rang a handbell as a signal for the pupils to get in line and march into the classroom. On cold days desks were moved around the pot bellied stove, where hot chocolate was served on Fridays, Older children helped the younger ones. Lessons were heard on a recitation bench.

Christmas programs were major productions. Names were drawn; Angel wings were made from coat hangers and crepe paper. Sheets were hung on wire for curtains with

safety pins which made a scraping noise as the curtains were opened and closed. I remember giggles behind the curtains, holly with red berries decorated the cedar Christmas tree along with popcorn and paper chains.

Probably the next most important holiday for the pupils was the Easter egg hunt.

The teacher was expected to spend the night in each home. I spent the night in one home where the roof leaked and the mother of the home had partitioned me a room using sheets. Children were on their best behavior when the teacher came to spend the night.

Winter came. I was walking up the road to keep the snow out of my face. I turned around and saw a man in a car backing down the road, He was trying to back into me without my seeing him.

It was in this little valley that I met the man who was later to become my husband. That was the best thing that happened to me that year.

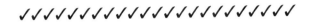

"I Didn't Miss A Thing"

After I finished elementary school, I wanted to go to high school. The closest high school was at Bland, Va., which was many miles away.

So the teacher, Mrs. Trula, who taught the one-room school, decided she would teach three of us the first year high school, after she had taught seven grades all day. We attended after school from 4-7 each day. Each of us paid her two dollars (yes $2.00) per month. This was six dollars per month for teaching three pupils who had completed the seventh grade the year before.

Miss Trula was an excellent teacher. She carried library and supplementary books in from other schools. She made books come alive. I can still remember scenes from Sir Walter Scott's *Lady of the Lake,* as well as many other classics.

The next three years I went to High School. Later I became valedictorian of my senior class. My not having my first year didn't seem to bother me. Because of a dedicated teacher I felt I hadn't missed a thing.

1980

"HE'S THE ONLY LITTLE BROTHER I HAVE"

Six-year-old Jennifer was in the back seat of the car holding year-old Nelson on her lap. They were on their way from Chapel Hill, NC to visit their Virginia grandparents.

Nelson was screaming. Mother said, "Jennifer if you'll quit holding him so tight he'll quit screaming."

Jennifer's reply," Mother, he's the only little brother I have and I 'm going to take good care of him."

"I DID THE BEST I COULD!"

Sometimes Grandmother talks when she should be quiet. She walked past four-year-old Nelson's bedroom and noticed that the bed was made. The sheet was hanging out from under the quilt, pillows out of line, and small footprints over top of the bedspread. Without thinking Grandmother said, "Who made this bed?"

Nelson walked up behind her about this time and said, "Grandmother, I did the best I could."

Grandmother thought about her big mouth and said, "Thank you, that's good enough for me."

''YOU BE THE JUDGE, LORD''

"My God shall supply all of your need..." (Philippians 4:19)

I had called Jerry to see how things on the job were going. She had experienced a trying week and was sobbing on the phone. It's difficult to try to calm people via telephone. After I hung up, I did the only thing I knew to do. I prayed. I asked God, if it was, his will, to cause her to get a bigger and better project than she had ever had before.

Time passed. Jerry was chosen to do the interiors of 199 villas in Saudi Arabia. And if that wasn't enough, the interior of the Hermitage Hotel in Nashville, TN. I began thinking, "What have I prayed for?" God is a big God. He is the first, to see our need. Sometimes, it's His wish that we have more that we ask for. All things are possible through prayer.

Later Jerry told me about how much work she had to do. It was then that I told her what I had done. I said, "The next time I'll pray, Lord, be the judge."

A Lesson on Dealing with Fear

It was great to be seated on the wagon beside my father. I sat quietly for a minute and let my eye wander, noticing the fragrance of the black-heart cherry tree in full bloom. My father noticed it too, threw back his head, laughed and began whistling a tune. He gently pulled one of my curls and said, "Don't be afraid, we're going to make it."

That was many years ago. On June 30, 1972, I crossed another stream. It happened like this.

Six years earlier June 12, 1966 to be exact my husband and I received a telephone call from Robert, our son-in-law, in Richmond telling us Jerry had a little girl. He also said there was something wrong with our granddaughter's heart. We soon learned that Jennifer Bancroft Law had been born with two holes in between the heart chambers. Her condition didn't get any better. She made regular visits to the Richmond Medical College for checkups. She didn't live a normal life for a growing girl.

When Jennifer was six, she was taken back to the hospital for the operation. She was well prepared and was not scared. As I look back, she was braver than either her parents or her grandparents. Packed along with the necessary items of clothing were one teddy bear named George and a pillow with a Smiley face on it, which she insisted on taking. She had carried the Smiley pillow for days before she left on the trip to the hospital.

When we arrived in Richmond, we found many sections of the city did not have drinking water due to a recent flood. The hospital had canceled operations for the next few days. This development didn't do anything to calm our fears. Finally the telephone rang and the voice told us to bring

Jennifer in. We did, all the while hoping for the very best for our little girl.

In preparation for the surgery a nurse brought in a little doll with tubes fastened to her and explained to Jennifer that when she awoke from the operations she'd have tubes fastened to her and look like this little doll.

We watched as they wheeled her away to the operating room. I told her stories those last few minutes. It was my way of handling the grief of the moment. The doctor said he would let us know as soon as the operation was over. We went upstairs to the lounge to wait. Later we went to a small chapel and we all talked to God. Open before us was a large Bible turned to Psalms 71. A verse stood out on the page, reaching out to us. "In Thee, O Lord, do I put my trust." I remember thinking, "Thank you, God."

After what seemed like days the doctor told us Jennifer had made it and that she would be all right. But she was in the intensive care unit and we couldn't see her for three days. On the third day, she came walking down the hall with the help of a nurse. This made our day.

There was no doubt in my mind that our Heavenly Father had helped us to cross successfully another swollen stream just like that time I was seated on the wagon beside my father all worried that we wouldn't be able to cross that body of water in front of us.

God Never Gives Up...

It was the first day of school. I was sitting at my desk in the office watching the pupils come in when I noticed in the doorway a small boy who was holding tightly to a little girl's arm. His clothes were rumpled, grimy, and his shoes were several sizes too large. His naturally curly hair was oily and unruly. They went to their rooms.

About that time, the primary teacher, Mrs. M. came in the office and said, "Mrs. Fox, I need to talk with you. I want to tell you about those two little children that just left out of here. The little boy has more real problems than a ninety-year old person should have. I thought you should know. They are foster children. The boy has been mistreated but nothing has been done about it. The girl is treated all right. Also, if the mother comes, don't let her scare you."

The next day I understood part of the warning. The mother arrived to pay for the lunches. She was dressed in her pajamas and her hair standing straight up, looked as if it had never been combed. Later I learned that the mother had a stroke.

I found Tommy to be a lovable but hyperactive child who cried a lot. He was in the second grade. He told me how his father, who was alcoholic, burned his hands with hot spoons and how he climbed to the top of the smokehouse to get away from him.

Tommy would surprise you by seeing deeply into a story. Yet much of the time he was too upset to study. He would bring pictures cut from catalogs and say they were his family. Time passed. Mrs. M and I went to a department store and bought him clothes and shoes to fit.

One day he asked Mrs. M if she would take him and let him be her little boy. I shall never forget Mrs. M going to the restroom; traces of tears still showed as she came out.

He came in one morning and showed us his back. Stripes crisscrossed where he had been beaten. I called the sheriff to come up and told him the story. He said, "Mrs. Fox, there's nothing I can do until a warrant is issued". There were tears in the eyes of the sheriff. He put his hand in his pocket and pulled out some money, "Buy him some ice cream until this runs out".

Not long after that, Tommy's foster grandmother secured a warrant for the father. The case was taken to court and the children were placed in the Custody of the Welfare Department. From there Tommy was placed in the home of a minister. He attended a different school and worked late hours after school selling flavoring for the church.

After Tommy came to Pearisburg to live, he began searching for my house. He did this by looking into people's mailboxes until he found my name. One day, he came up the walk, hugged me, and was so glad to see me. He had come from a neighbor's house. After looking at an artificial bowl of fruit on the table, he tried to eat the banana. When the neighbor told him it wasn't real, he said, "Don't you have a real one?"

It wasn't long until I heard that Tommy was under the care of a psychiatrist and was taking tranquilizers. About this time, a childless couple was looking for a child. Tommy was taken out of the home at Pearisburg and placed in their home. Later Mr. and Mrs. C adopted Tommy, loved him, and gave him many advantages. I watched him when he was in high school. He'd still hold his teacher's hand as he walked through the hall.

One day, in my classroom, I heard someone say, "Mrs. Fox". I looked around thinking it was one of my patrons. He said, "You don't know me, do you?" I recognized the voice and said, "Yes, you're Tommy". It was then that he told me, "I'm going to make a minister. I haven't told anyone but my grandmother. I wanted you and Mrs. M to be the first ones to know." From time to time he would come back to school to see me. A few eyebrows may have raised as Tommy hugged me or held my hand as we walked down the hall.

One day he came to my home and visited for a while. We talked of people we both knew. The next thing I heard, Tommy had a small church in Buchanan County. Three of us teachers and my husband went down one Sunday to hear Tommy preach. The sermon was simple but impressive.

Not long after this I received an invitation to his wedding. He was married at Hales Chapel, a church Tommy had attended near his new grandmother's home. It was a beautiful wedding. Recently, Tommy called and talked. He was excited about some of the things he had been doing; such as, being a minister, probation officer, and substitute teacher.

Currently, he is a minister in Holston Conference near Knoxville, Tennessee. This fall, he'll be working on his Master's Degree at the University of Tennessee.

Only those who really knew Tommy as a boy can appreciate this story and say with me, "It is true, God never gives up". (Tommy is now known as and is currently Dr. Thomas Conley, minister of Galax Methodist Church, Galax, VA.)

"TURN ABOUT'S FAIR PLAY"

Written for Jennifer's 14th birthday.

On June 12, 1966 I picked up the phone. A voice said, "Hey there, it's a girl. We have named her Jennifer Bancroft. "Bancroft?" I said, "What kind of name is that?" It's a family name that Jerry liked.

After packing my clothes quickly, I went down to Patsy Ann Drive in Richmond to stay with little Jennifer. "Why didn't you call her Patsy Ann?" "Ah Momma." It didn't take me long to discover that Jerry didn't think much of that idea!

She was red and wrinkled, tall and sweet. I stayed with her eight days, bathed, dressed and diapered her.

Jennifer remembered when she was in kindergarten. A see-saw had fallen on her big toe and crushed it. Grandmother had stayed with her again while the toe healed.

In Bishopville, SC she said to Grandmother Law, "I want to go and help Grandmother Fox, who has broken her leg." Papa met Jennifer at Roanoke, VA. Not knowing that Grandmother had played hopscotch when she was a little girl, Jennifer thought she did well hopping on her crutches. Grandmother called her Nurse Law.

Now Jennifer likes to make brownies, eat pizza, nurse Grandmother, visit with Phyllis next door, wash her hair every day, and talk with girl friends. "You know Grandmother, when I hurt my toe you stayed with me. Now I'm staying with you. We believe in taking turns, don't we?"

"WELL, DADDY!"

Rain had fallen heavily since sometime in the night. Papa had driven Jerry, a second grader, to school that morning. Around noon a flood warning was announced and the Mercer County schools were dismissed later in the day.

At 2:00 o'clock Papa had to walk over to the highway where he rode in a car pool to the Celanese on the 3-11 shift. While walking down the highway he looked ahead and saw two little people with an umbrella over their heads. Jerry was holding the umbrella over her little boy friend's head. She was embarrassed and said, "Well Daddy!"

DREAM COMES TRUE
FOR INTERIOR DESIGNER

Jerry Fox left home with a dream, to become an interior decorator, so called then, now known as interior designer. When Jerry arrived at Richmond Professional Institute she had very little money in the bank and had never been far from home. But she had her dream.

Today at age 36, Jerry Fox Law is the wife of Robert W. Law and the mother of Jennifer and Nelson, an interior designer, and president of Jerry Law Interiors. She has currently been chosen to plan the interior of the recently restored Hermitage Hotel in Nashville, Tennessee. (Later winning first place in the United States for Historic Restoration through the ASID, her professional organization, on this project) She is also designing and furnishing the interiors of 199 villas in Saudi Arabia.

Jerry had a difficult time learning to ride her tricycle. Her daddy hold her, "If you would get up to the table and eat your beans you could learn to ride it." She did, got down from the table and rode the tricycle. The need of confidence in herself had been what she needed.

Jerry, daughter of a textile worker and an elementary teacher, says the secret of her success is simple. "If you have a dream and if you really work at it you can make it happen." A philosophy she grew up on. Ever since Jerry was a little girl she wanted to be an interior decorator. As best she could remember the dream began about when she was ten years old and in the fifth grade. She took a 4-H project called Room Improvement and worked on her bedroom.

When she was fourteen her parents took her with them to a dinner at the Greenbriar Hotel. This impressed her greatly.

Jerry continued sewing and making improvements, especially in her bedroom.. One time she decorated her room in red, white and blue. The Home Economics teacher advised her to be an Home Ec. teacher. Her principal wrote in her high school annual, "She's little but don't underestimate her." Slowly her friends turned to other professions.

Her father offered to buy her a car if she would go to Concord College and stay at home. She said, "They don't teach what I want." So she went seeking her dream. At R.P.I. she spent her time earning her B.F.A. degree in interior design. Her first position was in Richmond, VA. She started out in an unfurnished apartment. Soon it was made livable with a camping cot for a sofa and a piece of plywood over a barrel for a dining table with art supplies stored in the barrel. After a few years in interior design she took the step for which everything else had been preparation. She began Interior Exports and started designing internationally.

Her biggest job, the designing of 199 villas for Saudi Arabia, is in the making. Jerry seems delighted but not surprised that she got her wish. Her mother and father were both from farms and they helped prepare her for hard work. The farm was a place where everybody worked. You worked until you got the job done. If you saw a rain coming you worked that much harder to get the hay in before the rain fell.

Now Jerry is a firm believer in the saying, "you can if you think you can." and " Be careful about what you dream, for dreams have a way of coming true."

I CAN DO IT

It was a hot July day, five-year-old Nelson had been asking his grandfather if he could go fishing.

So Grandfather took a water hose and curled it around making a circle on the ground and placed the hose in the back yard. "Son," he said to Nelson, "I'm not taking you fishing until you learn how to cast. Whenever you can stand here next to the porch and throw the line inside that water hose I'll take you fishing".

Nelson practiced and practiced. Two hours later he came in, perspiration dripping off his face. "I can do it," he said.

Grandfather looked at Grandmother and said, "We are going to have to take this boy fishing." They got into the truck and drive up to the pools at Willowton. Nelson began casting. He cast all the way across the pool.

Two teenage boys were there and one said to another, " Did you see that little boy cast?"

It wasn't long until a fish nibbled his bait. Nelson caught it. Then he caught another one and another until he had caught seven fish. He was so excited. "Man, what a whopper," he said, "good thing we brought Papa's truck so we can carry them home."

THE WATCH

(In Memory of Armistice Day, November 11)

I remember hearing my father tell this story when I was a little girl. Background for story is taken from the letters he wrote my mother while in service in World War I.

Few people expected to see American troops go to Europe. Wiley and his wife, Clara, had gone to housekeeping in a little house at Round Bottom (so named because of the round bottom in which it was located.)

On November 16, 1917, Wiley entered the Army and was sent to Camp Lee, Virginia. From there he went to Camp Greene, North Carolina where he found Clara a place to stay and she boarded in the home of an older couple outside the camp.

All this time Wiley was fortunate in having a friend, Meek, who was also from Tazewell County, just across the mountain from where he grew up. Meek always carried with him a gold watch that his father had given him. They were placed in Company L, 38th Infantry. Wiley wrote to Clara telling her that the flu had killed more than the war had and in the latter part of 1917, he wrote, "I think by Christmas there will be peace and doubt if I'll have to go across."

On December 28, 1917 he wrote, "I think the war will be over by spring." January 1918 found him at Camp Murritt, New Jersey. Clara went back to her parents' home at Rocky Gap. April 1918 found Wiley in France. The American troops had landed at Brest. He wrote to Clara telling her he was a doughboy now and to keep the home fires burning. "Time", he said, "is six hours different from your time. Meek and I will make it okay." While at home, Clara was humming "Over There", which was being played on the phonograph.

It went, "Over there, over there, send the word, send the word, to prepare, That the Yanks are coming, come, come coming everywhere...". The 38th Infantry was sent to Chateau Thierry to relieve the tired Frenchman. All through the summer months of 1918 Wiley and Meek fought in trenches with shell holes all around.

One morning Meek looked up at Wiley and said, "I have the feeling that I won't be coming back today. I want you to keep this watch." Wiley replied, "You'll see. Hang in there. Before long we'll both be back in Tazewell County. I'll be planting spuds on my side of Rich Mountain and you'll be planting spuds on the other side."

Clara had no idea when Wiley would be discharged, but she had a dream. She had dreamed that she saw Wiley in his uniform coming down the road. The creek was up with water overflowing its banks. But she ran across the footlog to meet him.

Meanwhile Wiley had been wounded in France and was on his way back to the States on the USS Huron. The newsletter published on the ship said, "Thanks, soldiers. We hope you will always meet with kindness and hospitality wherever you go. It is the opinion of every man on the Huron that a man who has been to the front and has done his bit, done all he can for his country, deserves everything we can give him and we hope that others you will meet will have the same opinion."

September 20th (Wiley's birthday) found him in Ward 26 in an Army hospital in Rahway, New Jersey. He had been wounded in the leg and the hand. Two fingers were missing from his left hand. A silver plate was placed in his left leg. He still had Meek's watch with him, as Meek did not come back that day.

Wiley was homesick. He wrote, "On my birthday some nurses tried to grease my nose, but I was like the squirrel the Irishman shot at. If you have a sharp pair of scissors, I wish you would send them to me so I can cut some of this red tape. When I do get to come home, I'll come to Bluefield and walk across the mountain. But don't meet me with any horses. I have been acquainted with a soldier's pack and can do 20 miles in 3-1/2 hours".

Armistice was signed on November 11, 1918 while Wiley was still in the hospital. He hoped he'd be home by Christmas. He wrote Clara and told her to be sure to kill one of their turkeys for Christmas because her parents, Sally and Will, had been so good to both of them. Wiley's presents remained unopened and he spent his Christmas in the hospital. People living around the hospital invited the veterans to their homes for Christmas dinner. Wiley enjoyed the dinner but missed being with Clara. Finally, the red tape was cut and on January 14, 1919, Wiley was discharged. He still carried Meek's watch.

It was pouring the rain; Clara looked up the road experienced the most beautiful surprise she had every had. Wiley, wearing his uniform was coming down the road. She ran across the foot log and up the road to meet him.

Soon after that on the other side of the mountain, a horse and its rider were galloping up the main road. Neighbors stuck out their heads and said, "That's Meek Devors. Nobody else rides a horse like that." Meek had been missing in action but now he had come home.

Weeks later, Wiley heard the good news and said, "Clara, I'll hitch up the buggy and we'll go to see Meek. I want to return his watch." Neil was hitched to the buggy and away they went.

As the two met, Wiley said, "It'll soon be potato planting time" Meet agreed.

The Work
and
The Reward

The dogwood had begun to bloom, showing the farmers that it was corn-planting time.

Early one morning, three of us, my sister Ruth, my brother William and I followed Daddy and old Nell, the horse, to the cornfield. After the ground was laid off and Daddy used the corn planter to plant the corn, we dropped the beans and pumpkin seeds.

We always argued over who got to plant the beans. They were slick and would slip out of your hands easier than the pumpkin seeds. So we took turns planting the bean seed, but everybody had to plant pumpkin seeds. Daddy would say, just as his father told him, to drop three seeds in a hill, but if you dropped four not to stoop and pick it up. But if you dropped five to stoop and pick it up.

He'd tell us to try to keep up with the plow. That meant we were getting the work done as fast as we could.

One day my brother got tired of dropping his pumpkin seeds. He found a rock pile and poured the seeds in the rock pile. Ruth and I didn't tell on him, we were tired, too. Summer came and the rock pile was covered with yellow pumpkin blooms. I remember Daddy saying, "To be sure, your sins will find you out". My brother never tried that prank anymore.

When the corn was up and about four inches tall, we began hoeing it. The rows were usually around the hillside; some were longer than the others were. My brother hoed the shortest row, he was the youngest, my sister the next shortest and I hoed the longest, since I was the oldest. If we rested too long on our hoe, Daddy would say, "That hoe has rested long enough". Then he'd tell us if we could step on our shadow, it was time to go to dinner or lunch as it is called now. We would try but fail. After a while we thought he took pity on us and told us it was time to go to dinner. We'd hurry off the hill to the house. I can remember being so hot and tired that it was a treat to lie on the linoleum floor and feel the coolness until Mother called us to eat.

Mother would work all morning getting us a good meal, trying to fix dishes each of us liked and usually a custard pie, which my father enjoyed. Nothing came from a can, unless it was something she had canned. Peas were gathered from the garden and shelled. Everything was first gathered, then prepared.

After lunch, we rested a bit and were ready to go again. The corn had to be hoed three times. Most every year, we hoed it four times, finishing before the fourth of July. The poplar trees around the cornfield would be in bloom, resembling yellow tulips. When the fourth of July came, we laid the corn by, which means we didn't hoe it anymore.

Then Daddy would treat us to a reward, which was a tour through a mountain cave. I don't know why he did this, but I accepted it at the time and never asked questions. It may have been that he had enjoyed going in the cave when he was a little boy.

There were no girls in his family, only three brothers. Four boys could possibly think of a lot of things to get into.

Anyway when the corn was laid by, he'd take us into a cave which was on his uncle's farm. You had to slide down for several feet, but before you reached one level of the cave through not too large of an opening. The cave was probably made by an underground stream, which flowed through openings in the rocks and made them larger. The things seen in the cave were formed in limestone by the

147

water, which trickled through the cracks and dissolves or wears away the stone. We would carry two lanterns and a rope so we could follow the rope back out. Once inside we saw beautiful stalactites joined together to form columns of stone. Some of these looked like curtains against the wall of the cave. One place looked like a wishing well without the pennies.

Another room was called the cemetery. The stones were so realistic, looked as if they were erected at the head and foot of the grave. We never tarried long in this area. The exploring was fun at the time we did it and we looked forward to doing it once each year.

But there came a time when I heard about Floyd Collins, a man who discovered Crystal Cave in Mammoth Cave National Park in Kentucky in 1917. In 1925, he lost his life while exploring it. Inside the cave is his tomb. After hearing this and realizing the danger I never went back again. Soon after that, the cave was closed with a huge boulder and large rocks.

BLACKIE

I heard my master say, "Midnight will have to go." I didn't understand what he meant but the next day I was taken into the mountains and left. My master got back into his car and drove away. I trotted down the road whenever night overtook me. During the day I had found a dump where, if I was lucky, I found a bite of food. My pads were weary. I felt that I couldn't go on without the friendship of another human being. So I decided to pick out an owner.

Then I heard a car passing. A lady with a soft voice said, "Look at that little dog. It's so thin that every rib shows through its skin. Somebody has dropped her." How I wished she could be my owner, but the car went on. Finally I reached a red cabin. There was no one around. It seemed such a friendly place that I stayed around. One day a car came to the cabin. The lady and her husband got out and went in the cabin. It was the same lady I had seem in the car. Soon she came out with some food and called to me. The voice attracted me but I did not go to get the food until after she went inside.

Time went on and each time the lady came she brought me some food and called to me. I still stayed about a block away. Later when she went inside I would eat the food and run away. The lady seemed friendly but I was afraid. Having no plan, I decided to stay around. From time to time I could hear people talking. The lady kept bringing me food and I kept getting closer to her. One day, as she was pulling weeds around the chimney I decided she was all right. So I pretended to stumble and rubbed against her ankles. She looked surprised and leaned down and rubbed her hand along my back, Then she cradled me gently in her arms. She had strong, good hands and I wagged my tail. It was then I knew everything was going to be all right. She

149

gave me a piece of bread. I held it in my mouth. I must have looked funny.

Then I heard them say they were leaving. I quickly scurried around and jumped up into the car seat, sitting as close to her as I could. When her husband got in the car I barked at him and curled up to the lady. The lady said, "Now what do you want me to do with you, little one? OK, I'll take you along." Soon the car began to shake and rumble.

My fate was uncertain, but it couldn't be much worse than what I had been through. The man turned out a street and stopped. Could this be home? My former master had not been good to me so I didn't trust this man and barked at him. For awhile I kept him outside the house.

Then I decided he looked kind enough and allowed him to go in. I whimpered softly and wagged my tail. The lady said, "Nice little terrier" So I was a terrier. Then she said, "I am going to call you Blackie." From that time on I was called Blackie. For several nights I slept on the front porch, which was made of concrete, under the lady's window.

Then one day the lady's husband made me a dog house. The dog house was at the back of the house and I slept in it. How I loved my new home!"

The lady seemed to know I had longed for affection. I met her each day as she came in from work. She was as happy to see me as I was to see her. I had found me a home.

FRISKY

It was love at first sight. I saw him lying at the top of the steps. We never knew where he came from. Each morning he greeted us with his paws outstretched to shake hands, his tail wagging and grunting a happy sound.

Each morning thereafter I was assured of a friendly handshake, before I entered the school building to teach the fourth and fifth graders. One little boy said, " You are a frisky thing." Another said, "He needs a name. Let's call him Frisky." And Frisky it was.

The children divided their lunches and saw that Frisky was fed. This went on for several weeks. Winter was coming. The children and I were concerned about Frisky. We had inquired about him. No one claimed or wanted a big shepherd dog like Frisky. Previously I had tried to teach the boys and girls not to pet strange dogs for they could get bitten. By this time it was clear Frisky had no intention of biting anyone and had made a liar out of me. The children agreed that Frisky belonged to us and that it would be all right for me to take him and find him a home before winter set in.

One day as I was going to the car I said, "Come on, Frisky". I opened the back car door and Frisky jumped in. I imagined I could feel his breath on the back of my neck as I drove. I had never ridden with an enormous dog in the back seat. I kept telling myself , "He has always been a friendly dog."

I had not thought about what I would do with him until I arrived home. I put him in the basement and closed the door. He seemed well satisfied. Then I baked a large pan of corn bread and gave him some to eat. My next problem was finding him a home. After I talked to my brother, who lived on a farm, he agreed to take Frisky and give him a home.

Frisky loved the farm, accepted my brother as his master, and in return for food and shelter guarded the farm equipment. One time he stayed on the truck with the equipment, without the driver knowing he was there. When the driver, who had borrowed the truck and equipment, arrived at his destination he thought a strange dog had jumped up on the back of the truck. He tried to make the dog get down but Frisky refused to leave the truck bed.

When the driver came back and stopped the truck at the service station, Frisky saw his master behind the counter. He jumped across the counter to join his master. The driver said, " So that's your dog; no wonder he would not leave the truck." Frisky continued to be a good guard dog.

At last Frisky had a good home. When I visited he would come with outstretched paws. I found that it took so little to make Frisky happy and he gave back so much.

LINKED BY STITCHES

"How did you happen to become interested in quilts?" I've been asked. I can understand why the question keeps surfacing. I usually have one in the frames, one cut out ready to go and another in the planning stage.

My answer is, "I grew up with quilts." My mother had quilts. She put the people around the quilt that could quilt best and the others in the kitchen to prepare the meal. Sometimes the quilt got finished in a day. She'd let me quilt a square.

My next interest developed after I was married. I began a hobby of collecting quilt patterns, books, quilt magazines, and articles. It was at this time that I made a Double Wedding Ring, which I learned was not an easy one for a beginner. Highly imaginative names were used for patterns which have always fascinated me, names for every conceivable reason such as Four Patch (formed of four squares set together). Many little girls learned to sew this one. Some named for the Bible are Job's Troubles, Tree of Life, and Robbing Peter to Pay Paul. Names of flowers, customs, tools, objects and way of life are also used. That's part of why I enjoy quilts, but the answer to the question of how I became interested in quilts reaches farther back than what I have related, as far back as Great Aunt Margaret's own family history.

Her full name was Emily Margaret Stowers. Aunt Margaret was my Grandmother Christina's younger sister. She was the ninth of eleven children, born in 1860. George, her oldest brother served in the Company F, 45th Regiment in Ferber's Brigade in the War Between the States. Wiley, just older than Margaret, had died young. Some of Margaret's older sisters were married and away from home before Margaret was born. Years passed and John married a minister's daughter, Susan Smith, and Nancy married Henry Belcher. Margaret remained at home with her parents, Colby and Lottie. Colby was born in 1822 and Lottie in 1824. Colby's grandfather, Mordica, was one of four brothers who were the first four brothers to settle in Bland County.

Great Grandmother Lottie was typical of women settlers. She had her own garden and canned enough vegetables to feed her husband and children through the long winter months. She raised chickens, milked the family cow, made her own soap, and made quilts to ward off drafts of cold that seeped through the cracks of her log house. She was accustomed to hardships and hard work was familiar to her.

Sometime during the 1860's, Lottie and Margaret pieced a quilt called Cross in the Square. According to a book entitled, "American Patchwork Quilt", by Lenice Ingram Bacon, these quilts were popular during the 1860s, the first known one having been made by a Bidwell family in 1859. Both Lottie and Margaret took pride in the blending of the scraps they had. A pleasant sense of achievement with each block suggested that time of life. When the squares were finished and joined into a quilt, they dyed the lining with walnut hulls, making a rich brown color.

Margaret must have helped some with the quilting. Girls at that time, by the age of ten, were ready to make their first quilt. The frames, cumbersome and space consuming, were suspended from the ceiling. Lottie and Margaret basted lining, filler, and fabric into place. They sat at the edge of the frame and reached forward to quilt the space in front, in rows of repetitive fans. In their split-bottomed chairs, they quilted with a disregard for time.

Margaret's sister, Christina (my grandmother), was five years older than Margaret. She married William H. Stowers and her first child was a boy who was named Wiley (my father), named after the Wiley who had died. It is said that Margaret loved this little curly, black-headed boy more than she did any of her own brothers and sisters. He was only six years old when she died at the age of 37. Before she died, she requested that my dad was to have everything she had, but if his first child was a girl, to name the girl for her and to give all belongings to that girl, me. I was named Beulah Margaret. When I was born, I already had a bed, a Bible, and a quilt. The quilt was the beautiful Cross in the Square, joined with a soft rose print with dark brown lining. The lining has faded into a tan color.

There has been a quilt revival the past few years. Some people like to look at quilts and some people like to make them. I like to do both.

Going back to the question asked me, I'll have to say that I believe that my love for quilts had roots in another century. I still have the quilt and someday will pass it on so that others may enjoy it as much as I have.

COLD, HUNGRY & TIRED!

Greg loved to fish.

He hadn't been at the cabin too long before he, his Mom, Dad, and Uncle Elmer went fishing.

He caught several fish.

Then he waded out in the water.

His feet slipped. He fell into the water, "I'm wet, I'm cold, I'm hungry and I'm tired," he said.

"That's enough for me, let's go to the cabin," Uncle Elmer said.

Molasses

Making molasses required plenty of patience and long hours. The cane grew from seeds since early spring and required a hot summer to thrive.

Early in the fall when the light frost began to nip, it was time to strip the leaves or blades. If the blades are frostbitten, the molasses have a bitter taste. But once the blades are stripped, the frost doesn't hurt.

We dressed as though it was winter to keep the blades from cutting our arms. We pulled downward on the blades jerking them off, a job I disliked.

After the blades were stripped the cane was cut with a corn cutter. Then, after they were topped of seedpods, the stalks were hauled by wagon to the cane mill. The seedpods were fed to the chickens. The cane was run through a two-roller press that squeezed the cane stalks causing the juice to run through a spout into a tub topped with a cloth strainer.

The juice was then poured into a large pan, which held about seventy-five gallons. The pan set on a rock foundation with an opening at one end to insert long pieces of firewood. The wood kept the liquid burning until about 5 hours later when the juice became molasses.

Tin with holes mounted on long handles was used to remove the skimming on top. The secret to good molasses was to keep skimming. As the juice began to thicken, it formed large bubbles knows as "pig eyes". When these bubbles burst, they set off a large amount of white steam. It wasn't long then till the molasses was ready. Neighbors dropped by to taste and talk.

I remember one time when the molasses was cooked too long and went into taffy. The molasses was too thick to be used so it was poured into the edge of the creek. We kids pulled off our shoes and waded barefoot through the

157

gooey mess. What a time we had squeezing the taffy between our toes.

The liquid was allowed to cool overnight and was ready to be poured into jars in the morning. It had taken nine gallons of juice to make one gallon of molasses.

For breakfast we could have buckwheat cakes topped with molasses.

My Grandmother, Sarah Christina Stowers 1855-1936

Monday morning as I hung my clothes on the line to dry, I thought of Christina. She was my Grandmother. Come Hell or High Water, she always washed on Monday, washing on the board all day long.

Before she did this she made her own soap. First a hole was bored in the bottom of a wooden barrel; then the barrel was set on a bench. Some straw was placed in the barrel with fresh wood ashes on top of the straw. When the barrel was nearly full of ashes, water was poured over the ashes. A brown liquid would drip out the hole. This was the lye she needed to make the family's soap. She would test it to see if it was strong enough by dipping a feather in it. If it ate the feather, it was strong enough. When a mother came visiting her with a baby or small child the mother would usually visit at our house and bathe the child. Grandmother never guessed what was going on.

Hollyhocks, lilacs, snowballs and day lilies surrounded her house, which was L-shaped and which was never allowed to be painted. She thought if her house was painted all of the preachers would stop for dinner. She always laughed when she said this.

She probably fed more ministers than anyone around and they always enjoyed going to her house.

The church record, which was transcribed by the Reverend S. K. Byrd, June 3, 1887 shows that she joined Mount Nebo Methodist Church sometime prior to this date, her name being the 28th name of this early church record. She never missed a service unless she was too sick to attend.

She'd put on her best dress, a new blue gingham apron, her best bonnet tied under her chin, and her high topped shoes. A safety pin seemed to be present at the neck of her dress. Then she rode horseback on a sidesaddle to church. To get to the church, she had to ride around a hill, which rose abruptly on the other side of the creek. This path wound around by chestnut trees – full of chestnuts in the fall of the year – and it led to a small white church on the very top of the hill. She always sat on the front row. "What's the use of a body going to church if a body has to sit back so far she can't hear?" When she got happy, and this was almost every time, she would shout. As she shouted, her bonnet would come off and go back over the crowd toward the rear of the church. There she talked with God asking him to save sinners. I can remember as many as a dozen coming forward at one time to accept Grandma's savior.

In looking back now I know she wasn't only my Grandmother, she was my friend. I enjoyed helping her. I can remember being sent to the cellar, which was about a block from the house, for cans of fruits and vegetables. She always called it the apple house. The door was so thick and heavy that it was all I could do to get the key to work and the door pushed open so I could get the things she wanted. Once inside, there was a certain predictable odor, probably coming from the apples.

She had a little meal room joining the kitchen. In the meal room were barrels and barrels of flour and meal along two sides of the room made from wheat and corn raised on the hillside farm. On the walls were shelves supported by spools strung on a metal rod. Across the end of the wall were gourds of different sizes with round holes cut in front. In the gourds were ingredients for making bread. Many times I watched her go in, turn around a time or two, and come out with a pan full of biscuits ready to go in the oven. She could make biscuits faster than anyone I know about. She never used any baking powder in her biscuits because she thought it was bad for the stomach. The biscuits raised more in the center than anywhere else. Along with this she might have chicken and dumplings, which seemed to be her specialty, hot raspberry pie, honey in a square dish, baked melons, brown sugar syrup and a pound of country butter. I never remembered eating there without the brown sugar syrup or the peaked biscuits.

One of my fondest memories is going to her house for buttermilk to make bread. She had a stone churn setting behind the stove full of cream ready to churn. She dipped in the churn and brought out about a quart of sour cream, "Here, take this home and make you some good bread."

One time, when her son was getting married, she said, "Go tell your mother to come over here. Randall is going to jump the broomstick." I ran home and asked Mother what jumping the broomstick meant.

There was always a lot of patching to do. That was where the spools came from. She never wasted anything. Yet that big heart of hers was just as generous as could be if she could share something with someone who needed it. When she patched anything dark she used white thread. When she patched anything light, she used black thread. I think she could see her work better that way. She never wore glasses.

One time she had a hen to steal her nest out and bring in one little chicken. Winter was coming on. Instead of bringing the chicken inside, she took care of it. She looked over at me and said, "Go fetch my scissors and the overall patches." I obeyed. She looked at the chicken and then she cut and sewed a garment to fit it. There may have been other chickens hatched late in the fall but I bet this was the only chicken in Clear Fork Valley that wore a neat little pair of overalls. I can't remember whether the chicken survived or not, but knowing Grandmother, I would say it probably did.

Grandma would say, "Beulah, can you spend the night

with me?" My bedroom was in a little bedroom joining the big room. In the winter she would heat irons, put them to my feet and then tuck me in for there was no fire in the bedrooms. I still like my feet tucked in.

I would sit for hours while she hooked rugs. Rugs overlapped each other in her living room, which was called the big room never the parlor. Regardless of the number she had she continued hooking rugs, while the five big clocks on the fireplace mantle in the big room went on ticking. They were never quite together, one ticking and then another. One was never allowed to run down.

You've heard of "kissing cousins". One day one of Grandma's cousins from Nebraska came to see her. The man called her Aunt Christina and put his arm around her. She slapped his face and said, "Now God I say, no stranger is going to do me that way."

As far as I know, Grandma was never more than 20 miles from home nor had she ever been to school a day in her life. She had learned to count to twelve from counting eggs and kept her butter and egg money in a tin syrup can in the corner cupboard.

One day, Grandpa left early one morning with his hired hands to work in the field without cutting any stove wood. They came in for lunch but there was no lunch. Without saying a work, Grandpa got busy and cut some wood. Then Grandma prepared the noon meal. From then on she had plenty of wood.

When God made her, He threw the pattern away. Her uniqueness only caused me to love her more.

My First Teaching Experience

I began teaching in the fall of 1938. I was 19 years old and had completed two years of college at Hiwassee, Madisonville, Tennessee. When a new teacher began teaching, she was sent to one of two places. Little Creek or Grapefield. Little Creek, I think, is near Wytheville, Virginia. I was sent to Grapefield.

There was a small post office there at that time. I believe the school board considered these two places to be good testing grounds. If you survived that first year, you were ready to teach anywhere.

My school was a one-room school. I enrolled 45 pupils, Grades 1-7. Water was carried from a well. There were two outdoor toilets behind the school, one for the boys and one for the girls. My students and I built fires in our stove, swept the floor and cleaned the building.

I had room and board with a good family who charged me $10 a month. My salary was $65 per month. I went home on the weekends. It was expected that I spend the night at each pupil's home. I did. I spent the night at one home where the mother had partitioned me a room using sheets. The roof leaked that night.

At another place where I stayed the lady of the house packed my lunch. At lunchtime I found twelve soda biscuits. Most of them had apple butter on them. I ate one and left the others in my lunch bucket. The lady where I boarded said, "What in the world are you doing with all the biscuits in your lunch?" She laughed when I told her what had happened.

Winter came. I was backing up the road to keep the snow out of my face. I turned around and saw a man backing down the road. He was trying to back into me without me seeing him.

One day I looked out the window and saw "Papa" riding on top of a load of hay. He had told the driver to go by the school windows.

It was in this community that I met your grandfather. That was the nicest thing that happened to me that year.

Part Three
Poems

Our Mulberry Tree

The first time I saw you was in July.
We were searching for a house to buy.
Elmer liked the house; I liked the mountain.
Jerry said, "Oh, what a beautiful tree."

We bought the house partly because of you, Tree.
You looked as if you had stood there for many a year.
Your limbs were twisted and gnarled.
I wonder how many picked berries from your boughs.

Or how many have rested in your shade,
Or under your branches have prayed,
How many have stopped to admire you
And felt your broad leaves wet with dew.

To a shift worker you were worth your weight in gold
As you provided shade untold
You are held together by wire.
Through the years your limbs and branches have died and
were cut away.
You were a handy thing for homes of birds and children's
swings.

Replacing your foliage now we see
A blaze of red roses climbing you
Using you as a trellis with bark as a perfect background.
So you could continue giving joy to each passerby.
You are more beautiful than ever!
(At 304 French Street, Pearisburg VA)

To
Jennifer 1982

You
remind me
of a tiny bud
with a chance to grow
in warm surroundings
in a flower garden
not bound by border.

You made it through the wind
gained strength
shared the sunshine
and rain,
unfolded
into full bloom
like the flowers
in Grandmother's flower garden.

Happy Sixteenth Birthday!

"Simple Pleasures"

(In Loving Memory of William H. Stowers, 1922-1982)

Bound to the earth with ties of blood,
He didn't have too little; he didn't have too much.
He seldom took a pleasure trip,
Used his moments in helping others,
Thought they were the finest folks, and asked for no re-
ward,
"No Charge," he said, "Come to see me."

Upon an autumn day
He was up and moving before the sun had topped the hill.
With the freedom of the meadows,
Like a boy, he climbed on his three-wheeler.

Used fertilizer and love
He sowed a lot of seeds,
They sprouted.
Grew.

He liked the rustle of the cornstalks
That took deep root in the soil.
The season's work was almost done,

Corn was gathered in,
Stored in an abandoned school building,
Cellar, granary and bin.

When the wagons were full
Nearly reaching the sky,
Moment by moment the whole day through,
With God in his heart, he sang a song
To the fertile soil, because the weather was fine.

He had a right to live,
To work,
To be himself.
Hauled the corn over ribbons of country road
That curve and wind.
Visited while he worked,
His neighbors understood.
The liked to chat a bit,
Shared their sorrow and their grief.
They had grown together in the soil,
Honest toil,
Work well done!

Sharp, clear Autumn,
Gave its color bright
The sun had dropped,

Left behind a copper glow.
Evening brought him home
To love and rest.

He had said, "Come".
The people remembered.
A stream of people,
All ages,
Came.

Hearts in rhythm,
Filed past a bank of flowers,
In upturned overalls,
Sport shirts
Suits and ties,
Straight from the fields,
Where the cattle were coming.

Around the hill,
The factories,
And town,
Talking of crops, calves,
Politics, and prices.
It's time the corn is hauled away.
Bringing $2.75 a bushel.
Hope tomorrow won't bring rain.
Maybe it'll be brighter.

Children
Touched his hand
And studied him
As if memorizing a poem.

In our hurried work today
Would that life be secure from greed!
So much is missed along the way,
A blade of grass,
Blessed rain,
Woods,
Fields,
Villages and streams.
Smiles, laughter of children,
Deeds of kindness
Cheerful, helpful neighbors.
Spring, Summer,
Fall, and Winter.
Gentle touch of the hand of a friend,
Trust in one another,
Unselfish gift of time and deed.
Solid, plain, steady things come slower.

Lord,
Today sweet memories linger.

The day is growing late.
Teach me the value of little things.
Let me be a Giver.

Help me to put the best that's in me there,
To know this land of mine has beauty,
To love this precious earth.
To realize that seeds must be planted in the furrow
Before they can take root and grow.

It's only the farmers
Who plant seeds in the Spring,
That reap a harvest in Autumn
From each little seed
That is sown.

There's many a needed help
That one can do or give.
Often it's the little things
That fill the greatest need.

What is Life ?

What is life
but a patchwork quilt?

With a craving for beauty
Made of bits and pieces
Both light and dark
Sewn together with grief
and laughter
To suit ourselves
Creating a unique design.

(May 8, 1981) ...Mountain Laurel
...Won Honorable mention in Annual Senior Citizen's Poetry Contest 1981...

Stowers Reunion

1982 *(In appreciation of Bob and Nettie Stowers, whose dream was to bring us together)*

In the gray hours of dawn 354 years ago
With gleams in their eyes,
Dreams in their hearts
And courage to spare.

Nicholas and Amy Stowers set sail
In a tiny boat, Abigail.
From Dorsetshire, England
Arrived in New England in early fall
To become the town herdsman.
And parents of:
Richard, Joseph, Abigail, Johanna, John, Sarah and
Elizabeth.

Today, July 4, 1982 on our country's 206 birthday
Their descendants, an endless stream of people of varied
ages
With gleams in their eyes
Came from the valleys, deserts, mountains prairies, and
coast land.

From the coal mines, farms, stores, factories, hospitals,
classrooms, garages and pulpits.

From Cummings, Skyline, Nater, Dawsonville, Nitro,
Dahlonega, West Hartin, Powatan, Myra, Hamlin, Netrie,
Pearisburg, Collinsville, St. Albans, Rocky Gap, Atkins,
Bluefield, Bland, Freedom, Crossville, Atlanta, Sacramento,
Los Angeles, Great Falls, Frankfort, Sepalveda, Palemo,
Elwood, Big Creek, Kirkland, Shady Springs, Joppa, Sid,

Huntington, Lavalette, Dallas, Alum Creek, Rudy,
Powellton, Danville, Peck's Mill, Logan, Switzer,
Richwood, Buchanan, Charlottesville, Hurricane, Groves
Road, Strawplains, Madison, East Liverpool, Youngstown,
Woodbridge, North Highland, Yawkey, Pleasant Hill and
Turtle Creek.
To join together for picnic and chatter

In precious time.
To Remember
And uphold their heritage.

They scattered
Richer than when they came,
As the rain stirred the tall trees.

Surprise!

Standing
on my crutches
I looked
into the tree.

And saw red roses
peeping in at me.

What Can
We Give You
for Your Birthday, 1981?

Since you have a Cadillac
Diamonds and fur.
This year we'd like to give you
Some extra special things.

Time (500 hours more or less)
Spent in the construction of
Cathedral windows in a quilt from
Miniature flowers
Set in a brilliant background
Of red, yellow and green.

Sight
Sky of softest blue
Children at play
Squirrel in a big oak tree
Freckled field of daises
Dogwoods in bloom.
Wild flowers blooming in the woods
Spider's web of crocheted lace

The sparkle of a dew drop on a blade of grass
Brilliance of the sunset
Glow from the church steeple.

175

Sound of
Wind whispering in the trees
Raindrops falling
Song of birds.

Smell of
Fragrance of mountain pines
New mown hay
Warm scent of fresh plowed earth.

Feel of
A quiet peaceful evening
A friendly hand in time of need
The coolness of nightfall.

These simple things our Father has loaned us
And we can share them with you.
Happy Birthday !

An Angel With A Rose

A small angel pin
Came in the mail.
Holding in her hand
A large red rose.

Ruth Stowers Heaton
With the angel pinned to gown.
Dreaming of her roses
And if they're bedded down.

Outside hundreds of bushes
Underneath a blanket of snow.
Waiting for the springtime
When they could bloom and grow.

Inside she dreams of a heavenly garden
Where flowers always grow.
Where she can walk among the roses.
An angel with a rose!

Sarah

A wee knock sounded on my door
"I brought you a flower".
She handed me a dandelion.
Limp from too much squeezing
And dropped her head.

Watched while I quilted
Reached out her arms and said,
"I've got to go now.
I need to give you a kiss and a hug!"
Then the brown-eyed bit of sunshine
Left behind a ray
As she hurried out the door.

TO MY AUNT

I am sleeping in your bed
Where you slept as a girl.
The headboard carved like an antique butter printer
Is the same as 120 years ago.

The climbing rose blooms outside my cabin window
The bank slopes to the water.
Through a gap in the trees
I can see the river.

Granddaddy says, there's work to be done.
I rise at daybreak to help with the chores.
As I sit by the warmth of the fire,
World of space and computers seem far away.
Time stands still at the river.

(Written for Nelson when he slept in his great, great, great aunt's bed. Summer 1981)

Blackberry Picking

Memories tug at my mind
Like brambles
Tore at my sleeves
on a sunny afternoon.

Dressed as though it were winter
Through tangles and thickets
To find black swollen jewels
One in my bucket
Two in my mouth

A bucket full of fruit.

❧ Ruth ❧

She loved her family, church and roses.
Knew each one by name.
She and God were partners.
Through the sunshine and the rain.

She knew her help
Came from Him.
She didn't have to work alone.
God was there for her.
She used her gift for Him.

Just like her roses
She had many names.
Some called her Ruthie
Some called her Mama Ruth.
Some called her Mom.
Her neighbors called her Friend.

God called her Special
And took her home to be with him.
Where she can walk among the flowers
And the roses once again.

SNOOPY

1985

You lived in a small log cabin
Painted brown.
You were used to be moved around
And had a friend with which to sleep.

I looked into your room
Closed the door softly
When I saw your shiny black eyes
Looking up at me.
Your ears drooping
And red tongue hanging out
Lying as if you never expected
to move again.
I thought I heard you say,
"Why doesn't Nelson come around"?

The Auction

I journeyed back today to the ground
where I was born
For sale at auction the paper said.
The pink ramblers were stubborn
They didn't know that the barn
and porch had quit
Brambles and weeds peeped
in the windows and the two front doors.

The crows gathered.
The stranger said,
"How much am I to bid?"
27 acres of farm and pasture.
More I could have told
It hurt to go too close.
So I stood behind the crowd.

My memories
Raked in long wind rows toppled over
Like shocks of new mown hay.
I smelled the fresh cut grass
and the spice wood.
We used to sweep the yard in Spring.

Birds sang in the blackheart
cherry tree
The brook was as clear as glass.
Peppermint grew in the water,
Red and gold columbine on the cliff.

And locust blossoms picked
for a bouquet
Placed in the center

of an oil-cloth covered table
My father had made from a walnut tree.

Gazed at the pregnant rock
in the foundation of the house
At the deep hole where I caught my first fish.
Called the trees in the orchard by names.
Saw the clothes Mother had hung
On the fence to dry.
The irises and rhubarb beside the garden fence.
The onion patch full of orange poppies
And white beehives with stump foundations
Along the yard fence.

The scene changed.
Bright bits of sunshine made a lacy pattern on the floor.
Curtains blew gently out the open windows
Custards cooled on the kitchen table.
I heard the auctioneer ask for the second bid
I had stolen the priceless thing
Right from under his nose
And he never missed a thing
As I turned and walked away.

(July 15, 1982)

Christmas 1981

A time of giving
to our children
grandchildren
relatives
friends
people we do not know
without expectation
in remembrance
of the supreme gift
God gave us
on that long-ago night
in Bethlehem
when the star shown
above the stable.

The shepherds
watched their sheep
Out of the East
came wise men
bearing gifts
to the tiny baby
giving from their hearts
the best.

We, too,
carry with us
the glow
of the star
the candlelight
and the tinsel
when we give
of ourselves
at Christmas.

Stacy and Holly

Effervescent laughter
Long blonde hair
Hand in hand
Two little sisters
Stacy and Holly.

Took care of each other
Made mud pies
Did the dishes
Straightened the room
Fed the ducks
Gathered the eggs.

Whispered:
"You tell her."
Then together said,
"1, 2, 3
Thank you
For the cookies.

(June 1981)

To George, Who Went Away

You are gone.
The feeling rushes over me
Like the tide.
You hike no more the moist earth
Or judge the roses in the show.
You teach no longer Sunday school
You are gone.

You went away.
Oh God, who is it then that walks through my mind.
When I see a Boy Scout
Or children who need some clothes?
Could it be that goodness
Like ripples made from stones.
Keeps widening and is never lost?
Surely, now as always
You are here!

Grandma

Wrinkled face with clear blue eyes
Silver hair that wandered out of place
Round rag rugs hooked by the fireplace
Competing clocks on the mantle piece
I remember Grandma
I tore the strips of cloth.

Hollyhocks dressed in red, pink and white
Grandma standing in front
Having her first picture taken
I remember Grandma
I took the picture.

Orange day lilies and lilacs by the porch
Purple morning glories around stalks of corn
Big permelons hanging on the vine
I remember Grandma
I carried in the harvest.

Homemade lye soap
Out of ashes, water and fat
Carried to the smokehouse
And put into a vat
I remember Grandma
I cut out the cakes of soap.

Grandma going into the pantry
Gourds used for canisters
Containing flour, soda, and salt
Yellow peaked biscuits covered with
brown sugar, syrup and butter
I remember Grandma
I ate the biscuits.
(1981)

Strong Love

Mary was the farmer
Joe, the hired hand.
Who came to Mary's house
To repair things on the farm.
And became her spouse
Joe constructed a log house.

They stuck together through the lean years.
Sixty years later they're still here.
Two old people not able to help each other.
Hoping to get a little stronger
Trying to hold on a little longer.
Love is strong.

The Old Dinner Pail

Out in the garage
high on a nail
hangs my father's old dinner pail.
With a wire handle
and a tin cup
that fits on top.
As I saw it,
memories leapfrogged
through my mind.
I saw Mother
bringing it
up the hill
at noon.
Cornbread and vegetables
in the bottom.
Fried apple pies
in the tray.
A gallon of milk
in a White House vinegar jar.

One more row of corn to hoe
then we could eat.
Sitting underneath the poplar tree
Scattered with yellow tulips

That cast lazy shadows
in the corner of the rail fence.

Free to talk
while muscles relaxed
to dream
of swimming
in the deep hole
fishing
playing house
and exploring the cave
when the corn was laid by.
A memento speaking softly
of a part of my life.

6-5-84

To Hince and Gladie

6/14/84 (for their 65th Wedding Anniversary)

"Come, come to our house
Come spend the day or a week."
As you stop us
On the street.

Time, like precious jewels
Is given to neighbors and friends.
As you go
Along the way.

You live a life of giving
Find joy in simple things.
Laughter of your grandchildren
The crimson sun at the end of the day.

It's just that in your heart I know
You're truly sweet and kind.
You have a smile for everyone
And leave good thoughts behind.

Happy 65th Anniversary!

To One Who Went Away

You are Gone!
The feeling rushes over me like the tide.
You plow no more the moist earth or weed
the strawberries by the road.
Your eyes no longer turn homeward at sunset.
You, my oldest brother, who used to play with me.
You are Gone!

You are Gone!
Oh God, who is it then that romps and plays in my
dreams.
And walks through my mind
When I give his cakes away?
Could it be that goodness like ripples made from
stones
Keep widening in the heart and is never lost.

2-15-83 (In Memory of my brother William Hicks Stowers)

Spring Cleaning

April morning
Things to do
Discard
Sweep
Dust
Polish
Freshen
Organize
Asked God to help me
spring clean my soul.
I needed to
Discard unkind thoughts
Sweep out misunderstandings
Dust off cobwebs of neglect
Polish with God's love
Freshen with new experience
Organize my time
To spring clean in April.

Gratitude

September 10, 1980
I'd look out and see you there
You called it getting sawdust in your hair.
The ring of the saw was music to my ears
For out of the wood something beautiful
would appear.

We sat on your porch and talked
about the weather
It was a treat, all of us together.
You had a philosophy that wouldn't quit
You always said, "Don't worry about it".

You carried my meal when I needed to eat
For a good neighbor, you could not be beat.
You enjoyed doing for others
I have no doubt.
You believed that's what life
was all about!

I'm thankful for the gifts you gave me
And all the things you made me.
Memories keep coming without end.
But, most of all, I'm thankful
I had you for a friend!

Love is Something You Can't Buy

"They're not for sale."
I heard him say.
A duck that wobbled,
flipped and flopped.
A jumping jack that performed
magic tricks.
A man that climbed a rope
and slid right back.
Reaching out he gave her the toy
"It's the bestest gift I've every had."
Come over here and let me give you a hug,
she said.
Her wide-eyed face so young and bright.
He found his job in little things
with no thought of recompense or price.
His reward came from what he gave away.

Toymaker.

Heirloom

With the coming of Spring
An isolated woman
Figured, measured, and checked
Watched quaint designs grow
Under busy fingers.

Rectangular hardwood frame
Suspended from ceiling
Held in place with pegs
Lining, filler and fabric
Basted into place.

Afternoon sun cast a shadow
on her work
As she sat at the edge of the frame
Reached forward to quilt
the space in front
Along the line of the design
Marked in soft chalk lines
Rows of repetitive fans.

Engrossed in work
In a split bottom chair
Created a textile sandwich
With disregard of time
Made a Log Cabin patchwork quilt
To ward off drafts of cold.

BEGINNING TEACHER

September 7, 1938
A brand new teacher
At the age of nineteen.
Assigned to a school
She had never seen.

Two years of college
Where she needed four.
Thrown into Wolf Creek
To see if she could swim.

At a school called Grapefield
Where practice began.
Walked two miles a day
Carried books and biscuits.

Opened at nine
Closed at four.
Stayed another half hour
To sweep the floor.

Gathered pine knots
Built the fires.
And carried water from the well.
Two toilets out back

Salary sixty-five dollars a month
Ten dollars room and board.
Home on weekends
Rang a hand bell signal
For pupils to line up
In front of steps and march into classroom.

On cold days
Moved seats
Around the pot-bellied stove
Where hot chocolate was served on Fridays.

Older children helped younger ones.
Lessons heard
On a Recitation bench.

Christmas program
Major production.
Angel wings
Made from coat hangers
And crepe paper.
Sheets hung on wire for curtains
With safety pins.
Scraping noise
As curtains closed.
Giggles behind the curtains.
Holly with red berries
Cedar tree
Decorated with popcorn and paper chains.
Names drawn.

Laughter
Easter egg hunt
Prizes for the most eggs.
Spent nights with pupils in rooms
Partitioned by sheets.
Where roofs leaked
Teacher and pupils
Learned from each other.

JUNE 1980

No way I'll forget June 1980. I stepped in a ditch while attending a yard sale which resulted in a fractured knee. A cast was on from hip to ankle.

Jennifer wrote on the cast....

Grandmother, so sorry you hurt your knee.
At least you're taking it with glee.
But please don't go to any more yards sales for me.

Grandmother added her own verse which said....

I'll obey your request with deep regret. For I haven't finished my shopping yet....

Aunt Margaret's Quilt

Rare old quilt of faded hue
I'd like to know more about you.
I know Aunt Margaret promised my Dad
She'd make him the prettiest quilt he's ever had.

She said, "Today, I'll start a quilt for you.
I'll make it of patches, red white, and blue."

Dad watched the gentle hands
Stitch by stitch sewing the scraps of calico.
She used pieces both light and dark
And some of cheerful hue.
One scrap was great Grandmother's Lottie's dress.
And one was Uncle Isaac's shirt of blue.

With patience, skill and pride,
Day after day the pattern grew.
She dyed the lining with walnut hulls
Because it was the thing to do.

This wonderful quilt reflects history's past.
Each scrap is a printed page.
It warmed the heart of a little boy
And gave to him a lot of joy.

There is a message hidden here
Made of love and dreams and thread.
There were no radios, automobiles or TV's,
So she stitched her pleasures instead.

W.G.H.

(With God's Help)

I am a tenant
On this earth.
Walking barefooted
Through the fertile soil.

On my journey
The world presses in.
I remember the letters
W.G.H. means With God's Help
He takes my burdens
And lightens my spirit.